T0316430

CORPORATE WRONGDOING AND THE ART OF THE ACCUSATION

CORPORATE WRONGDOING AND THE ART OF THE ACCUSATION

Robert R. Faulkner

ANTHEM PRESS
LONDON · NEW YORK · DELHI

Anthem Press
An imprint of Wimbledon Publishing Company
www.anthempress.com

This edition first published in UK and USA 2011
by ANTHEM PRESS
75-76 Blackfriars Road, London SE1 8HA, UK
or P O Box 9779, London SW19 7ZG, UK
and
244 Madison Ave. #116, New York, NY 10016, USA

British Library Cataloguing in Publication Data
A catalogue record for this book is available from the British Library.

Library of Congress Cataloging-in-Publication Data
Faulkner, Robert R.
Corporate wrongdoing and the art of the accusation / Robert R. Faulkner.
p. cm.
Includes bibliographical references and index.
ISBN 978-0-85728-791-5 (hardback : alk. paper) – ISBN 978-0-85728-794-6
(pbk. : alk. paper)
1. Corporations–Corrupt practices. 2. Business ethics. I. Title.
HV6768.F38 2011
174'.4–dc23
2011020949

ISBN-13: 978 0 85728 791 5 (Hbk)
ISBN-10: 0 85728 791 5 (Hbk)

ISBN-13: 978 0 85728 794 6 (Pbk)
ISBN-10: 0 85728 794 X (Pbk)

This title is also available as an eBook.

For Howie

Contents

Acknowledgments

I would like to show my appreciation for the valuable critiques and helpful recommendations offered by Wayne E. Baker, Blair Bigelow, Eric A. Cheney, Joe Cobbs, David Cort, Donald T. Tomaskovic-Devey, David Grazian, Gil Geis, Sarah O'Keefe, Anna Kacperczyk, Mark Parent, Gerald M. Platt, Andy Papachristos, John Walton, Lawrence S. Zacharias, Brian Guzzi and Ezra Zuckerman. I am also grateful for the generous assistance offered by Lindsay Carvalho, Andy Cerow, Jason Ferenc, Michael Morand, Michael Marotto and all of the "corporate crime gang," for their help in the "keyword sleuthing" and in the preparation of the corporate "hits list." Special thanks are due to Professor Krzysztof Konecki, for encouraging the writing of an earlier version of 'The Dean's Lecture' (Institute of Economics and Sociology at the University of Lodz). I would also like to thank Izabela Saffray and her colleagues at the Centre Michel Foucault, Recherche en Sciences Sociales, Université de Varsovie for their generosity. Professor Pawel Starosta, Dean of the Faculty of Economy and Sociology at Lodz University, Poland, provided critical support for the early stages of the project. A preliminary report on the subject of this text is "Repertuary przestepstw gospodarczych," which has been translated into English for publication as: "Repertoires of Wrongdoing in Markets" (Wydzial Ekonomiczno-Socjologiczny, Uniwersytetu Lodzkieg). I owe a special thanks to the *New York Times*, for permission to quote from articles featured in their business section, and I also wish to acknowledge the help of the editorial staff at Anthem Press, particularly the careful assistance of Robert Reddick and the overall support and encouragement of Janka Romero.

My deepest gratitude, as always, is to Laura and Olivia, my daughters, who, despite busy lives of their own, found the serenity to put up with me. They suffered through my attempts to formulate ideas about culture and economic exchange, then dug in and helped sharpen the entangled and complex coding of the accusations as event cases, facilitated the organization of the data file, and most importantly they kept Daddy laughing and loose. The initial inspiration for embarking on this venture came from Howie "The Count" Becker, who contributed sharp insights into the moral order of markets and accusations as collective action; dedicating this volume to him expresses a token of my indebtedness.

1
Accusations: Between the Innuendo and the Illegal

C'est plus qu'un crime, c'est une faute.

Trust, honesty, and integrity are the principles upon which our financial markets function. Americans don't hate large corporations and rich executives, but they do despise those who behave as if the principles don't apply to them. The ferocity of this reaction should not surprise us.

Public accusations of misconduct are indications of how much antipathy there is towards miscreant manufacturers, bankers and other executives who don't play fair, and large, publicly traded corporations that violate the code of conduct that is supposed to guide economic behavior. The devious and underhanded violation of this code raises red flags of warning, throws an unwanted public spotlight on managers and management, leads to increased railing against bad corporate practices, reveals the negative sentiments of accusers about specific market exchanges in goods, services, and investments, and undermines the confidence of American citizens in the integrity of the market.

Accusations of wrongdoing and railing against bad corporate management and managers occur well before the law is invoked, before criminal indictments are handed down, and before people are sentenced. The techniques used by rating agencies, the fancy dressing up of quarterly financial statements by banks, bogus balance sheets, misappropriation of investor capital, and, generally, outright fraud and deception by top-level corporate management, normally relegated to the shadows of finance,

1

can also include creative accounting techniques, which mislead rating agencies, dupe suppliers, buyers, and regulators, mask deteriorating finances – overall, artful combinations of lying, stealing, cheating, and concealing.

Outspoken critics of corporations, investment banks, hedge funds, and rating agencies spend years trying to get people to pay attention to potential fraud, investor rip-offs, and tax evasion of large firms. Not only did they try to get people to pay attention to the failures of rating agencies before the recent financial crisis became full-blown, but they called the staff at the agencies "jerks," "worthless," the investments "make-believe" and "utter garbage," and the crowd that relied on the agencies as not only "certified idiots" and "the brain dead," but the investors and adopter organizations who relied on the ratings as acting like "lemmings," or in an esoteric vein, as "agents without principles," and even more harsh, as "schmucks."

The blows always start with rebukes, accusations, finger pointing, and red-flag warnings. Railing against the regulators, the rating agencies, and the large corporations, along with finding those responsible for wrongdoing is an enduring feature of capitalist society. When economic action goes awry, and buyers or sellers or investors are wronged, harsh words help them hone their point. They are not afraid to use them. Such emotions are nothing new, but in socioeconomic affairs during the 1980s they seem to have started to boil over. What once played out beyond earshot of the trading floor, the buyer-supplier contract grievance hearing, the boardroom, or the law office has become very public: the tangled, uneasy, and often antagonistic relationship between a corporation and its suppliers, buyers, peers, analysts, rating agencies, and regulators.

This breach of the code of the market uncovers the taken-for-granted assumptions of socioeconomic behavior. Moreover, such public announcements as revelations of wrongdoing in economic life are not random. Nor are they the idiosyncratic behavior of a small group of wayward corporations and their executives. Rather, they are ordered. As such they help reveal the working constitution of the market as an institution.

For the past twenty years the media have reported about large, publicly traded industrial corporations, hedge funds, accounting firms, ratings agencies, and investment banks accused not only of mistaken assertions (or, if you prefer, lies) and misappropriations (or embezzling, looting, or stealing), but also misdirection of capital (through bribery, kickbacks, and payoffs). Corporations and their executives have also been accused of making promises they never intended to keep, while breaking the rules protecting free-market capitalism.

Breaking the rules undermines the trust upon which markets and their participants rely. In making purchasing decisions, for example, buyers rely on the truthfulness of representations made by sellers. In making pricing and production decisions, industry rivals vie for the business of buyers and rely on their competitors to play tough, but fair, and not engage in bribery or coercion of customers. In making financial decisions, investors rely heavily upon the integrity of corporate financial reports prepared in accordance with accepted accounting standards.

For connoisseurs of financial wrongdoing, fraud and blunders by corporations still hold a key place, with a focus on consumer- and investor-based cases that affect people's everyday financial lives – their stock portfolios, pension funds, mortgages, credit cards, and ultimately their confidence and trust in markets. Fraud is only one part of the story. Insider trading schemes, Ponzi schemes, and "perp walks" by Wall Street traders receive photo coverage in the *New York Times*, *Washington Post*, and *Los Angeles Times*. We've seen Lehman, Bear Stearns, Wachovia, Washington Mutual, Countrywide blow up along with banner headlines and television coverage of prominent financial companies accused of misleading and cheating their clients. Analysts and lawyers on Wall Street misused their privileged positions of fiduciary responsibility through lying and looting. There were suspicions and buzz about Henry Blodgett and other high-profile securities analysts potentially hyping stocks to curry favor with their banking firms' corporate clients.

The media's narrative of abuse and portrayals of corporate villains are red flags or early warning signals that something went wrong in market-based transactions between corporations and their customers or clients, suppliers, peers, analysts, and regulators. Enron lied to its employees, to federal regulators, and misused its so-called special purpose entities to create "virtual sales" and "off balance sheet liabilities" to inflate its assets, make accounting statements look prettier, hide costs, and cook its books.

Commercial and military aircraft manufacturer Boeing bribed its way to several multimillion-dollar contracts with public sector work and the Pentagon. Payoffs were a line item, a way of life, and a normal cost of doing business at Siemens, the giant German industrial firm. Since late 2006 the Munich-based firm was embroiled in allegations that it paid bribes to government officials in order to win contracts on numerous projects.

In late 2009 New York attorney general Andrew Cuomo garnered banner headlines for his accusations about pay-to-play practices in which financial brokers and other middlemen use kickbacks and campaign contributions to gain access to retirement funds. Warning signs also went up at the same time at the California Public Employees' Retirement System (CalPERS) when it revealed it was conducting an internal review of the amount of money paid to a former board member for marketing money managers to the giant pension fund. The review by CalPERS was part of growing scrutiny by funds and authorities in several states, along with the Securities and Exchange Commission (SEC), concerning potentially improper practices in the way public pension funds make decisions about which money managers will get the lucrative contracts to manager state retirees' money.

And in the mundane world of baking cookies, the company called Archway & Mother's was accused of booking nonexistent sales and systematically logging sham transactions allowing Archway, owned by a private equity firm, to get access to badly needed capital from its lender, Wachovia.

The same kinds of allegations were made public (1) before the last market downdraft in 2000 to 2002, (2) during the revelations of the accounting scandals involving Enron, WorldCom, Adelphia Communications and Tyco, (3) during the 1980s in the junk bond and insider trading debacles with Drexel Burnham Lambert, Michael Milken, and Dennis Levine. and (4) during the late 1980s and early 1990s in warning signals sounded about Lincoln Savings and Loan, American Continental and Vernon Savings in influence peddling and gambling with depositors' insured funds preceding the calamity in the Savings and Loan industry. Executives of those institutions were accused of being engaged in wide-scale fraudulent practices.

Even earlier there were alarm bells about a reinsurance scam at the high-flying Equity Funding Life Insurance Corporation, suspicions of forgery and banking fraud at the successful leasing company called Other People's Money, the investment frauds by Richard Whitney (1938), Ivar Kreuger (1932), and Charles Ponzi (1920), and other scandals in a series stretching back to the Dutch tulip mania of the 1630s and probably beyond.

The viral signs of Wall Street's public scandals and investment swindles appear not just in the illegal trading of stocks (Whitney), matches

(Kruger), or postal reply coupons (Ponzi), or even in civil and criminal cases in which breaking the law has been proven and the guilty await the disposition of the case in settlements and sentencing. Long before the perp walks and before the prosecutor wins (or loses), murmurings of lying, cheating, and stealing stir under the surface, in innuendo, euphemistic assertion, gossip, and hearsay. This occurred a couple of years before Bernard Madoff's walk down the East Side surrounded by photographers and reporters, before his Ponzi scheme came to light, but around the time that a suspicious Wall Street watcher sent a letter or two to the Securities and Exchange Commission, urging regulators to look into potentially phony annual returns of Bernard L. Madoff Investment Securities LLC. He claimed there was something funny about the so-called "fund of funds." At that time, regulators made no inquires. In 2009 Madoff admitted to running a sixty billion dollar Ponzi scheme for years. The SEC was criticized for missing opportunities to uncover Bernard Madoff's massive fraud. They were also criticized for their lax oversight of Wall Street investment banks and lack of attention paid to concerns about stock market manipulation. Ironically, as early as 1999 the SEC was accused of missing the warning signs or initial accusations aired by Harry Markopolos, a securities industry executive and specialist in forensic accounting. Markopolos smelled a rat and started warning regulators about Madoff in 1999 and met with an SEC official in 2001. The SEC investigated Madoff in 2007 and didn't find any evidence that he was engaged in fraud. "Markopolos points out no less than 29 red flags in his statement to the SEC" (Manuel 2009) – this was in a nineteen-page document that Makopolos submitted to the SEC in November of 2005, titled "The World's Largest Hedge Fund is a Fraud."

In Chapter 2 we shall look in more detail at these so-called "red flags." We begin by describing the thing to be explained and identify important elements of a unifying framework. "Red flags" are accusations. When they are classified across several meaningful dimensions (e.g., the type of accusation such as lying, cheating, and stealing; the reasons for the misconduct; the rules that apply to a particular situation), we see the *assembly* of the accusation as a social act.

We are particularly interested in the actual corporate targets of public accusations, the market-based exchange routes on which these occur, and the distinctive keywords and catchphrases used in making the accusation. From this discussion we formulate expectations regarding what corporations on which exchange routes are likely to be accused.

Figure 1. Types of Corporate Wrongdoing

	Public Announcements	Criminal/Civil Violation
Innuendo	−	−
Admonition	−	+
Accusation	+	−
Indictment	+	+

+ = present; − = absent.

It is the combination of words and market-based transaction routes that is critical.

There are four types of announcements of wrongdoing: (1) private, in-group murmuring, gossip or *innuendo*, (2) private, in-group reprimand, reproach, or *admonition,* (3) public allegation, rebuke, or *accusation*, and (4) public, official, formal charge of criminal or civil rule violation, or *indictment*. See Figure 1 for a typology.

Innuendo is a veiled, oblique, and privately expressed statement that reflects on the character, reputation, or social status of the target. Gossip and slander are confined to a specific social circle; they are nonpublic expressions of discontent with the conduct of a person and while socially supported within the confines of the "in" group, they are often officially deplored. For example, an executive of a corporation is suspected of violating company policy by embezzling company funds. Insults and *sotto voce* murmurings circulate about an employee's abuse of trust and misuse of official position.

Admonition is a privately expressed warning or disapproval that reflects on the potentially criminal behavior of the offender. It is an injunction to refrain from doing a specific behavior. The behavior is defined as illegal or rule breaking. The matter is handled "discreetly" and behind the scenes, even though there are potential criminal violations or civil rule infractions involved, such as embezzlement, trading on nonpublic confidential information, or bribery and kickback.

For example, a corporation discovers an executive whose behavior violates not only company policy, but also criminal statutes as well. The matter, however, is discreetly handled in-house. Companies also sometimes delay providing information to the authorities in breach cases, fearing lost customers. In several instances we learned about from our informants, the employee may be "outplaced" to another firm and positive letters of recommendation may even be drafted on the employee's behalf. The person is neither sued nor is any public statement about the misconduct aired.

Accusation is a publicly expressed and perspicuous statement of alleged wrongdoing that affixes blame on the supposed offender. It is a strong, clear signal designed to restore social order; in the case of business, it seeks to redress a violation of company policy and the formal and informal rules governing the conduct of business. Unlike the private admonition, there is a public allegation of misconduct; the finger of blame is pointed at the culprit. But unlike the indictment, the accusation does *not* involve formal charges of criminal conduct. In the accusation, a business is picked out and served up as the "unacceptable face of capitalism" – a term coined by the late British prime minister Edward Heath. It taps into today's accusations.

Indictment is a publicly expressed, formal charge of criminal behavior against the offender. The finger pointing and blame is public. In addition, there may be allegations of criminal negligence, crimes of omission and commission, and violations of rules and regulations governing business transactions. For example, an executive of a corporation is publicly charged with grand larceny and the embezzlement or misappropriation of company funds. Or a US attorney hands down a criminal indictment alleging that the executive had been running a Ponzi scheme, and the SEC and the Commodities and Futures Trading Commission file civil suits charging that the executive had defrauded investors of nearly a billion dollars.

The four forms or kinds of allegations are interconnected, but distinct, social processes. Innuendo, admonition and accusation are laced with barbs and recriminations, reflecting the acid tenor of relations among the accused and accuser. There's no denying that they often slander and exclude others, extinguish trust, and provide guilty pleasures for onlookers and audiences. The reprimand may have the same bitterness of a business relationship gone sour. There may have been, in the example in the previous paragraph, murmurings that the executive used the incoming money to cover payments due to other, earlier investors, and that he also moved money out of their accounts and into accounts that he used to make speculative trades. Investors may have quietly conducted inquiries into these speculative trades and the uses and misuses of their accounts.

The admonition is private and utilitarian. The accusation is public and demonstrative. The indictment is public and always involves criminal and civil charges.

A distinctive feature of the accusation is its *in-betweenness*. With innuendo and insult on the informal side of making allegations and criminal indictment on the formal, legal side, the accusation stands astride the scathing cavil and the neutrally worded lawsuit, between privately assailing someone as a scoundrel, or deftly (and quietly) managing a rule-violating employee or publicly (and loudly) charging the employee with a crime.

The accusation is critical to the institution of the market because it is the initial, *public* warning signal about the improper business conduct of capital*ists* while revealing the potential threats to the system of capital*ism*. Why is the accusation a critical event in a market? Markets are collections of economic information, translated through trading into prices. They are also collections of social information, translated through communication into accorded reputation and status.

These prices, unless there is manipulation, are the best estimate of future supply and demand. These communications about reputation and social honor, unless there is lying, cheating and stealing, are the best estimates of future trust, transactions, and business contracts. Expressions of discontent, signals that the situation needs to be improved, are "danger ahead" warnings about the past – and often the recent past – behavior of trading partners in the market. In making an accusation we are making a statement to ourselves about the kind of people we are, and what we will not accept.

The accusation is a tool for evoking *unambiguously unfavorable symbols*. For a warning sign to blossom into a full-scale accusation, the key words and phrases surrounding the economic wrongdoing are stripped of their neutral connotations. For example, words such as "sharp business practices," "exaggerated claims," "cutting-edge trading," "speculative high-risk behavior," and "using cheap money to make risky loans and trades" can be viewed as depicting acceptable business conduct, fully in accord with the *mores* of socioeconomic behavior rather than variants of lying, looting, bribery, or the violation of trust. In an institution or "system that gives priority to the endless accumulation of capital" (Wallerstein 2004, 23), people and firms accumulate capital to accumulate more capital. Avarice is not, however, illegal. Favorable definitions of the pursuit of capital abound as long as the pursuit of it is within the mores. To enrich through deception is another matter. The breach can occur when there is an endless accumulation of capital by other means, for example, by siphoning off investor funds for your own personal use, by looting from the firm's coffers through quid pro quo arrangements with the chief financial officer, by forgery of financial statements, by collusion with industry peers. To the extent that the accused is seen behaving within the bounds of proper business behavior, albeit on the cutting edge, positive or neutral connotations will block more extreme and negative ones. To the degree the capitalist is perceived as crossing the line, we expect that fewer neutral connotations will characterize the corporate case at hand and that a preponderance of negative connotations will appear in the news, the specialized business press, and editorials and commentaries.

Accusations are shaped through four techniques: (1) focusing on a specific market-based tie, (2) stripping away connotations that are favorable and nuanced, (3) abbreviating or leveling the public denunciation into a concise message, and (4) attributing or casting explicit blame. When *focusing, stripping, abbreviating and attributing* occur together a principal theme emerges. When enacted together, the four create an "identifiable perpetrator" effect: a way to get people's attention is to focus publically on the person or the corporation's personnel who are benefiting from the wrongdoing, rather than on an amorphous group (such as "senior managers," "executives," "middle-level professionals," or "the industry," "lobbyists," "trade groups," etc.).

An essential to the art of assembling a public allegation is transforming implicit and neutral attributions of wrongdoing into explicit and negative ones. The accusation is shaped using these four techniques to shift from private murmurs and grumblings to the public sphere by means of fashioning and refashioning of the keywords, phrases, and memes. When the transformation is in the public sphere with *regularity* on market-based exchange paths, accusations become accusatorial repertoires in markets.

While the accuser may say it is just about business, it is always about much more. While many of the prominently reported *claims* boarder on the criminal – circumvention of antitrust laws and bribery of officials, for example – the majority of capitalism's public accusations are less about money and more about violations of unwritten agreements and broken promises. Money is always involved in markets, of course, but the market is a place in which lying, cheating, and stealing arouses exclusive and unfavorable feelings towards wrongdoers. Public reaction is always vitriolic. Rightly or wrongly, the accused is cast as engaging in "boldly deceptive conduct," "reprehensible" behavior, or having "reneged" on a pledge, as having broken a promise, and then having been the unrepentant beneficiary of ill-gotten gains.

For example, when Wiltron, a small maker of test equipment, accused Hewlett-Packard of violating antitrust laws in monopolizing the market for a type of microwave analysis equipment, it said that HP engaged in a range of "reprehensible, unlawful and coldly calculated" acts designed to "cripple" the firm's ability to compete. They also said that Hewlett-Packard "disparaged" Wiltron's products and offered "discriminatory price breaks" to selected customers. The company also said that HP "formed so-called SWAT teams" designed to "Stop Wiltron Advances Today" (Zonana 1988).

Traditional approaches to white-collar crime and corporate crime implicitly presuppose that formal charges of criminal wrongdoing tell us everything we need to know about violations of rules and regulations by the well-to-do and by those who own and manage large businesses. Events leading up to the charges may have helped create the conditions for the civil and criminal indictments, but once the criminal justice system is invoked and in play, the initial allegations have no further influence. In this view, the proper study of the moral order and deviance is the study of crime and law.

Our evidence from decades of accusations made in the public sphere suggests that this view of corporate conduct and moral order in America is incorrect. Durkheim ([1893] 1947, 102) suggested that the modern era would increasingly be characterized by the interplay of morality and crime, for "Crime brings together upright consciences and concentrates them." Erickson (1966) says, "The excitement generated by the crime...quickens the tempo of interaction in the group and creates a climate in which the private sentiments of many separate persons are fused together into a common sense of morality." Building on qualitative content analysis and quantitative analysis, our conclusions highlight ways in which crime and consciences are conjoined as Durkheim and Erickson suggest, yet our conclusions differ from those envisioned by them. We suggest that the often-accepted use of criminal indictment and formal charges may be weak rather than strong indicators of moral excitation, group sentiment, and "a common sense of morality." Rather, it is the public accusation of wrongdoing *preceding* the official criminal charges that generates the excitement, the tempo, and the sentiment that are assumed to underlie "the public temper" and the moral order. In our view, in white-collar and corporate crime, by the time the sentencing arrives, the aura of gravitas and moral seriousness is exhausted.

Nearly all of the contingencies and conditions of the moral "climate" and public outrage drawing people together, as viewed by Durkheim and other social theorists of moral order, occur before the arrival of the regulators and before the invoking of the criminal justice system in the form of civil complaints, the criminal investigations, and the formal charges. For example, as discussed above, whereas gossip faces little if any public scrutiny, the accusation is public and is always about alleged cheating, duplicity, and improper practices. It differs from the vague suspicion about rule breaking inside the firm, which can be sniffed out, scrutinized, and kept under wraps. It also differs from the ambiguous and anonymous accusation about bad behavior inside a social group. Unlike law, which seeks to establish facts and assumes innocence, the accusation claims grievous harm, defines a business situation wrong, and assumes guilt. For example, one technique of the accusation (attributing) casts the alleged wrongdoing in the most unfavorable and unambiguous light possible. Another technique is to make absolutely clear that a market-based transaction is clearly delineated in simple and understandable terms. Accusations can also borrow the language of the law and tailor the alleged wrongdoing to the transaction. This is not a one-size-fits-all enterprise by any means. As we shall argue, the concrete manifestation of these techniques are found in early red-flag warning signs found in media and news announcements referring to "blameworthy" corporations and their executives.

As a general rule, successful accusations are adapted from preexisting source material – but not slavishly. They exist in the so-called shadow of the law, but are not replicas of the law. For example, Bittner (1967, 702) argues that in many social disorder situations, responsible social actors (i.e., police on skid row) "not only refrain from invoking the law formally, but also employ alternative sanctions," ranging from warning offenders to "direct disciplining." The aim is to draw attention, to sharpen the framing of, and simplify the social connection between the wrongdoing and its wrongdoer. As we shall see, these stories of corporate wrongdoing are custom-made attributions of blame, rather than plain vanilla caricatures of law breaking. As the announcements are sharpened they lead to aggressive public airings of this connection as well as to revelations about many other things: the internal workings of a corporation and its managers, the firm's relationships with its stakeholders, and cozy ties to analysts who cover the firm as well as to investment bankers who help syndicate its merger and acquisition deals and underwrite its stock and bond offerings.

Accusations bring unwanted attention to the firm's dealings with its suppliers and customers, let alone its relationships with powerful politicians and government officials.The allegation is often a noisy and nasty disclosure – a revelation that cuts through the social silence of the taken-for-granted. It breaks away from the accepted and everyday muted grumblings about promises broken, or privately shared gripes about someone reneging on a commercial deal, or the gossip about sharp practices and self-dealing. The consequence not only is to bring the offense and the offender into the spotlight and to excite the collective imagination but to tailor the announcement to the specifics of the case at hand.

Allegations are admissions that capitalism isn't perfect. Commerce, finance, and credit are founded on trust that emphasizes fair dealing and honesty. The allegation exposes more than just the seamy side of markets and exchange; it is a critical social event saying that something's gone wrong, giving voice to a claim that the normative order has been violated. This normative order is the consensus about the behavior that is expected of the group members by each other. The trick is that it's not always what people say that contains the most important information; often, it's what they take for granted. And getting at what they take for granted is immensely difficult.

The accusation lifts the lid on the taken-for-granted-ness of markets by revealing what happens when expectations are violated. The accusation is that it seethes with indignation and yet is rational, that is, articulate and succinct. An accusation gives voice to a perceived violation of the social silence of the moral order. The public allegation, which the violation has provoked, can rejuvenate and affirm the very norms of taken-for–granted behavior that have been breached.

This book describes accusations: what they are, who is involved, what happens when they are announced, the feelings they arouse. It is also about how they reveal the culture of corporate business. Accusations are the middle ground between informal grievance and in-group gossip, between organizational and regulatory screening programs designed to ferret out suspicious economic activity on one side, and the formal processes of civil complaints, criminal investigations, enforcement, judgment, and sentencing on the other side. They also have a duality, publicly revealing the interweaving of market-based ties and the market's rules of conduct. We call this the dual nature of an institution, the interweaving of structure and culture (see Baker and Faulkner 2009). When they take hold, public allegations of wrongdoing, with their in-betweenness and duality, become exemplary social signals, dramatic communications about the breakdown of trust and the breach of rules of proper business practice.

A breach of the normative order evokes a wide variety of reactions. In production markets, corporations and their executives go beyond private squawking about the usual ruffles – the various forms of dissatisfaction perennially suffered in economic exchange – and go public. They stop the quiet complaining about the underhanded tactics and questionable business practices by their business associates and give public voice to their private dissatisfactions. Accusations straddle the two hemispheres between informal and private grievances over the noncontractual relations of business (Macaulay 1963) and formal and public complaints about contractual violations. Informal and private grievances are in the taken-for-granted agreements and unwritten agreements; formal and public complaints are in the glare of the public spotlight on potential criminal and civil action. The formal complaints evoke legal remedies by regulators and authorities in federal, state, and local institutions.

Much as we would like to explain corporate wrongdoing by making it strictly about the violation of the noncontractual *or* the contractual – promises broken or laws violated – it is usually a combination of the two that draws societal attention and action. The study of accusations is the study of the shift from private to public, the shift from informal grievances to formal allegations, for at this juncture the turning point in the career of an accusation occurs.

Because accusations are such a consequential part of organizational life, reaching a thorough understanding of their culture and structure is critical to elaborating accurate theories of organizations and markets. Social science research on corporate crime and misconduct has tended to overlook or gloss over the intermediate processes, or the points where the shift from noncontractual to contractual complaints occurs. Catching the process from different angles reveals the social gap that exists between the informal voicing of a complaint, grievance procedures (Coleman 1987; Edelman, Uggen and Erlanger 1999), and arrival of the charges in the form of a civil or criminal lawsuit. (Civil cases are often easier to win than criminal ones because the burden of proof is lower – preponderance of evidence, rather than beyond a reasonable doubt as in criminal trials.)

A public accusation of wrongdoing, though often described, is seldom taken systematically into account in the analysis of the rules governing economic relationship as they play out in routine business interactions. By focusing on the first announcements of the allegation – after the screening systems ferret out suspicious economic activity, after the in-gossip has secretly aired the wrongdoing – we discover the earliest, public breach of standards of right and wrong such as defrauding stakeholders, fraudulent financial reporting, violations of regulations, bribery, collusion, unfair business practices, and potentially criminal behavior. An otherwise quiet tolerance for a disregard of unwritten agreements can turn into a vocal, and loud, proclamation of resentment, recrimination, and rebuke. Giving voice to these complaints in the form of public accusations allows researchers to discover a few ideals to explain large masses of otherwise unintelligible, manifest data on corporate business behavior. Sometimes there is more whisper than voice. Allegations surface in discrete disclosures by firms and their regulators. A corporation may, for example, see that laws and regulations governing bribery or insider trading are going to be more strictly enforced and mount a concerted attempt to nail down wrongdoing in the corporate suites and managerial ranks, anticipate the government reaction to their potential law breaking and report it to the regulators, coming clean in hopes that the regulators will give them a break.

Accusations are in between informal grievances and formal charges of criminal or civil misconduct and even later, sentencing. Accusations of economic crime by big corporations reveal the seamy side of the American market. The market is an "institutionalized mechanism... which facilitates exchange" (Baker, Faulkner, and Fisher 1998), and so accusations of violating the rules of exchange play a dramatic – and at times controversial – role as danger-ahead warnings about the breakdown of trust and deterioration of confidence among business associates. As public proclamations, they openly affirm, by their very violation, the cultural standards of conduct governing business relationships. The accusatory event is rife with furor and finger pointing. The level of the furor and direction of the finger pointing helps reveals the nature of the accusation (what is alleged), its object (who is accused), its salience (how intense the furor is), and its patterning (where the dissatisfaction is distributed in market-based ties).

Trillions of business transactions every day make up our global economy. Ivy League academics, Wall Street analysts, Washington regulators, fund investors, corporate sellers, buyers, and competitors all assume that ideally, markets are based on truthfulness, reciprocity, and fairness. However, in reality, unscrupulous behavior such as fraud, deception, and bribery taint many business transactions. The ideal of shared trust and good faith breaks down when one side of a business transaction believes it has been victimized; it accuses the other side, the offender, of dishonesty, deception, cheating, stealing proprietary information, and opportunistically exploiting a business relationship. The cover of legality is taken off of the social mechanisms – trust, cooperation, and bargaining – that ordinarily govern socioeconomic market relationships.

As Emile Durkheim ([1912] 1995) argued, shared beliefs define reality. From money to law to business, a society's workings depend on shared views about what is proper and improper behavior. In profit-making organizations, business in general and markets in particular, shared ideas of right and wrong, ethical and unethical, go hand in hand with watching and reacting to competitors' economic behavior on price and volume (White 1981) as well as their commitments to the norms of appropriate institutional behavior in socioeconomic exchange (Macaulay 1963; Bradach and Eccles 1989; Levitt and Dwyer 2002).

The market is "a social institution which facilitates exchange" (Coase 1988, 8). The legal pursuit of market profits depends on institutionalized rules of the game and what sociologists call a social and cultural "context" (White 2002). What they mean by the market as a context is a culturally shared approach to observing key players in the market, the significant others, such as peers, rivals, competitors, and constructing categories and repertoires of economic action. Acutely and often anxiously sensitive to the posture, position, and intentions of other companies, monitoring each other constantly, companies are aware of changes not only in the market's immediate concerns of price and volume but also status and reputation.

Our point of departure is White's (1981) maxim: markets are publicly observable patterns of socioeconomic behavior. They are "social structures" of tangible activity. The activity occurs between corporations, and "among specific cliques of firms and other actors who evolve roles from observations of each other's behavior. [What] a firm does in a market is to watch the competition in terms of observables" (1988, 518). Among some of the most closely watched observables are sagging profits, sinking stock prices, and second-rate management. But nothing sullies a corporate reputation like a publicized revelation of fraud or bribery or collusion or other kinds of market misconduct. Why are these closely watched? Because amid the righteous indignation, Schadenfreude, and human-interest story, there is inherent drama, sensation, and even debate over what happened and why. Media announcements of alleged wrongdoing energize corporate and financial markets and their social actors. There are several features of note.

First, the accusation is a small spectacle. It is a small sign that the big, customary social order has broken down, at least for those involved in the market-based relationships. The event provides "the local public…insights into the everyday functioning" of the market that make accusations and allegations "a crucial resource in the empirical study of event-structuring processes" (Molotch and Lester 1974, 109–111; Warner and Molotch 1993).

Second, an accusation is a public portrayal of wrongdoing that deploys iconic claims and keywords in its "event-structuring process." These words define and refine an event in crisp, familiar, easily understood, and unambiguously negative terms. As noted, an accusation is an early warning, a danger-ahead signal of trouble. And it involves a redefining of the situation to find out not only what the wrong is, but also who is wronged and by whom. Inevitably, in this event-defining process the accused becomes an archetypal betrayer.

Third, the accusation is always highly charged. As opposed to the lengthy legal complaint by a federal or state regulator, or the formal brief filed by a complainant in a legal case, the accusation is short and highly condensed. Unlike the formal complaint or criminal charge, the accusation is shorn of legalistic details. The accusation is sharpened through the use of adjectives, provocative headlines, and dramatic story leads. There is never anything neutral about betrayal, about lying, stealing, and cheating in the market. Recriminations were directed at Enron, Tyco, Adelphia, Lehman, AIG, Washington Mutual, Countrywide, Wachovia, WorldCom, Parmalat, Siemens, Drexel, and HealthSouth. A writer from *Rolling Stone* rolled out the underwater metaphor for a major investment bank suspected of financial wrongdoing, likening it to a "great vampire squid wrapped around the face of humanity, relentlessly jamming its blood funnel into anything that smells like money."

Fourth, the accusation comes wrapped in a package. It is more than a publicly observable event involving the behavior of market competitors and participants gone wrong. It is an event expressed through catchphrases and keywords (Ghaziani and Ventressa 2005; Gamson and Modigliani 1987, 143). These catchphrases and keywords chronicle, capture, and classify "signature elements," framing and promoting definitions of "what happened," "who was involved," and "what went wrong," shaping the story and providing a theme. It is a symbolic packaging of a hotly contested market situation, a virtuoso exercise in the "redescription of behavior in order to transform its moral significance" (Machiavelli 1955, xxxiv; Skinner

1990; Baker 2005; Thomas and Znaniecki 1918). Symbolic packaging uses keywords "...is a frame...a central organizing idea...providing meaning to an unfolding strip of events" (Gamson and Modigliani 1987). The events unfold in the business community and in the general as well as the business press (Warner and Molotch 1993), alerting players in the market, and shaping the attention of other interested parties. And an accusation is a retrospective statement about the past. Now that the accusation is announced, everyone could have or should have seen the warning signs long ago. The looting of the firm was carried out under the noses of the board of directors, the complaints of fraud were ignored by federal regulators, the bribes were suspected and covered up for years, the buyers knew there was collusion but did nothing. In effect, warnings were missed. This has the tendency to step up the pace of paying attention. The accusation moves through the business world, the media, and the press at a fast tempo, changing the pace of life. "It is in the nature of a critical situation that the tempo of action is speeded up: choices which ordinarily can be postponed must be made immediately; conflicts which normally may be minimized and endured must suddenly be resolved" (Turner and Killian 1957, 45). It moves between the retrospective and the prospective, between the warnings missed in the past and the potential delegitimizing of the organization in the future.

We coin the term "double embeddedness" to denote the two-sided nature of accusations and their role in the market as an institution (Baker and Faulkner 2009). Cultural embeddedness and structural embeddedness and their interactions are variable, dynamic, and complex. Accusations charge cultural violations of the code of business and they are always found in market-based ties. It is a public response to perceived decline in the quality of the socioeconomic relationship between parties in the market. It is a communication saying that something has gone awry, and its public nature invariably follows the more informal name-calling, shouting, and attempts at shaming and social humiliation. It moves the discontent from informal disputation to public denouncement.

Orchestrating the accusation, as opposed to generating gossip or filing a criminal complaint, *is the art of the intermediate.* One side informally enunciates grievances and complaints; the other side formally announces charges of violations of laws, rules, and regulations – illegal conduct. The accusation stands between the informal and the formal. In socioeconomic market conduct, accusations are focused, abbreviated, and easily grasped accounts of unscrupulous business behavior. They are not cloaked in understatement or delicate euphemisms. They are concise and report a limited number of details but are neither civil nor criminal in their charges. The trademark of an accusation is that it can't be vague or speculative, like gossip and hearsay; it must be immediate and concrete, borrowing the language of a criminal indictment, but lush and prolific in attributing blame, stripping out neutral legal connotations, and honing in on the unwritten agreements underlying the specific market-based transaction.

Gossip involves "whispers," "small talk," "idle chatter," or "hearsay" and tends to be private and have an "inner-circleness" about it (Gluckman 1963). It is often meant to hurt people, and can be used to exclude and slander others, in a devious and underhanded manner. Accusations too can be meant to hurt, exclude, and slander others, but they are announced in public, often in the media and the press, before a general audience. Like rumors, accusations are public, but unlike rumors, which are ambiguous and speculative (Rosnow and Fine 1976; DiFonzo 2008), accusations are detailed and specific. They affix blame. They apply rules *in situ*, that is, to a concrete situation. They inform group members about how to act properly in a given situation. And accusations serve as a warning device motivated by social concerns.

They may eventually be filed as criminal or civil legal complaints, and they are with some regularity. But this outcome is neither inevitable nor predictable. The accusation occupies a dual social space: on one side we have the informal carping, quibbling, and dissatisfactions about business conduct among market actors; on the other side we have formal filings, investigations and subpoenas about potentially criminal or civil violations by the market actors. More generally, they can an also "cast a cloud over the firm," as the founder of a hedge fund recently said. He was facing accusations of insider trading and a long-running civil investigation by the SEC's lawyers (Zuckerman and Scannell 2009).

Seemingly small items of behavior can often betray the existence of larger phenomenon: seemingly minor broken promises becomes fraud, forceful efforts at persuasion becomes bribery, glossing over some fiduciary obligations turns into systematic looting of the firm, acceptable pilferage becomes theft, and protection of honored secrets becomes obstruction of justice. The shifting back and forth across these two regions – the informal on one side, and the formal criminal justice system on the other side – reveals the dynamics of the moral order of the market. Sociological analysis focuses on moments of tension and conflict like this, because that's when unexpected and intermediate events interrupt collective activities that ordinarily go unnoticed. They are the goldilocks of defining the mores of the market in critical situations.

Accusations are dramatic public declarations that become more coherent and consistent announcements of the events – business actions that interrupt or disturb the taken-for-granted assumptions and obligations of market-based conduct. They make us aware of what is going on in socioeconomic behavior between firms, for example, drawing attention to the taken-for-granted assumptions and expectations between firms in a market. On the one hand, accusations of violating the rules of the game can bring a corporation into an unwanted spotlight of negative publicity. "Bad news" can tarnish the reputation of a company, undermine its efforts to establish a distinctive identity, and raise suspicions about its future behavior. On the other hand, accusations can indicate the firm is innovative, is willing to take risks, and is not averse to pushing the envelope. Being bad may in fact be good for business, as reflected in the stock price of a company. An initial dip in the market's evaluation for some of the organizations we have studied is followed by recovery and sharp rise in the price. The market, it would appear, absorbs the news and reevaluates the future earnings of the firm in the light of the allegation. Being in between the legal and illegal can be advantageous for a firm. As one of our informants put it, "being accused of fraud, bribery, or deception may be just a cost of doing business and the market absorbs it."

Allegations can also lead to changes in a firm's accounting control system, to senior management shakeup and reorganization, to hiring outside lobbyists and other specialists, and to efforts to improve future cash flows. In this case, the disclosure of the "bad news" in accusations may be "good news" to the corporation as investors react positively to good faith efforts on the part of management to deal with the negatives surrounding an organization accused of economic wrongdoing. The market may initially react unfavorably to the first disclosures of defrauding of stakeholders, collusion, and rule violations (Karpoff and Lott 1993). Karpoff and Lott used the *Wall Street Journal* as their main source and found significant stock market reactions to disclosure of fraud by management. Allegations that reach backward into the past and forward into the future shape market participants' – customers, suppliers, lenders, credit raters and Wall Street analysts – ideas about unethical practices as well as the more local or specific illegal behaviors surrounding a firm (or a "clique of firms").

Public allegations of lying, cheating, stealing, and other "self-disbelieved statements" (Williamson 1975) indicate that someone has violated the rules of economic exchange. Rules of exchange are collective understandings about "who can transact with whom and the conditions under which transactions are carried out" (Fligstein 1996, 658). These rules govern, for example, the use of the "exit option" (Hirschman 1970), the ease and conditions with which buyers and/or sellers may exercise the modern right to break relationships (Coleman 1974). This right to break relationships exists as part of the cultural tools available to market actors, so does the right to voice complaints.

Opportunistic behavior is "any action engaged in by an exchange partner, enjoying an informational (or some other) advantage, to exploit that advantage to the economic determent of others" (Barney and Ouchi 1986, 19). Ironically, few scholars have explored the concepts of opportunism and economic crime in the area of social activity it came from, the sociology of markets and networks. It is here that we might expect thick description and rich analysis of illegitimate behavior and "the pipes and prisms of the market" (Podolny 2001). The empirical study of finding fault and making allegations offer important clues to the rules of exchange in a market, noting, of course, that the ideal rule and the rule in practice might be quite different.

Accusations come before formal, legal charges. One party finds fault with the behavior of another and then accuses the other of violating the norms of business conduct. Party X may dispute Party Y's actions (Galanter 1983), and Party X may say that Y has betrayed a relationship. Betrayal of trust are acts that "change the course and the meaning of relations between persons" by breaking economic ties and relationships, disappointing trusts or expectations, or negating memberships (Turnaturi 2007, 8).

The problem can be settled privately and quietly. A business rival accuses another company of competitive subterfuge. Buyers and sellers, for example, have a working arrangement based on certain understandings about proper business conduct. Party X decides that Party Y is doing something that is disadvantageous to him. He complains, tries to settle it "out of court," so to speak, and maybe Y sees the point, makes some readjustments, and all is well. Or Y gets recalcitrant, tells X off, and X feels aggrieved and accuses Y in some public way. Most of the time Y and X do not especially like airing their dirty laundry in public. They may figure there are harmless technical violations of ethics standards. At other times, however, X sees the matter as neither harmless nor amenable to private negotiation and then makes allegations of wrongdoing.

Accusations between buyers, sellers, and rival peers can be settled privately, but there can be noisy clashes which devolve into what sounds just like petty playground taunts, with allegations sounding like the economic equivalent of "you cheated me." Whether they are quiet or noisy, they reflect genuine outrage. Market actors may fight (Bourdieu and Wacquant 1992) in order to legitimate their claims, seeking retribution for misrepresented products and services, or revenge for self-dealing by a company's top-level executives. It may also be retaliation for broken promises and contracts with suppliers of professional services such as lawyers, accountants, appraisers, analysts, and other personnel essential to the workings of a company. And it may be a search for redress of a wrong, a vocal announcement that a firm is seeking a remedy for long-simmering conflicts between a company and its customers, clients, peers, and state and local regulators. Ugly stuff, in other words, and mightily entertaining.

The breadth and depth of allegations pull back the curtain on a dark and persistent problem in the nation's economy. Enron, WorldCom, Global Crossing, Kmart, Arthur Andersen, Qwest, HealthSouth. They are accused singly. They are accused in groups. They are accused and then fall with a heavy thud of bankruptcy, shareholders whipped up, stakeholders furious, investments analysts duped, employees laid off, families hurt. All this begins with allegations of wrongdoing. The sheer speed of these charges of wrongdoing is unnerving. Companies that are healthy just moments ago, it seems, are suddenly alleged to have not only engaged in human folly and excessive risk-taking, but to have committed economic crimes, industrial subterfuge, fraud, extortion, and violations of securities law. It seems as if a "success oriented" culture fosters a climate of unrealistic performance goals, pressures to excel and take risks, until the violations of the norms and standards of business *become* the standard.

What are the conditions under which these accusations occur? What are the legal environments of corporations (Edelman and Suchman 1997)? Are there patterned recipes of wrongdoing – accusations of committing acts that reasonable people would deem reprehensible, unsavory, or illegal? Are there organized ways of expressing dissatisfaction, consternation, anger, and fault with the economic behavior of the exchange partner? Where do these accusations of economic crime play out in the market? How are they distributed on what sociologists call the "market interface" involving interaction between vendors, clients, buyers, distributors, peers, investment analysts, bankers, brokers, and government regulators?

And in the aftermath following the announcements of the allegations of wrongdoing, how do corporations respond to the charges of unethical economic behavior by people acting within or on behalf of the corporation? Do they fire the boss? Sweep out the current senior management group? Reconfigure the board? Or do they head off or blunt the accusations by deploying Washington lobbyists, advertising firms, publicists, financial analysts, or public relations firms?

The principal themes behind allegations and reactions to those allegations reveals the culture of a market as a set of cognitive schema or recipes by which economic actors solve different problems, invariably about money, exchange, trade, bargaining, and reciprocity. Recipes are ways of understanding how market culture works. Recipes are activated in the course of corporate business; they are part of economic exchange; economic position in the market constrains and channels recipes. And thus, economic actors' ideas and understandings of legitimate and illegitimate behavior are shaped by their structural economic contexts.

What these public allegations share is a simple and clear narrative that captures the imagination of the market players as well as the general public. They tap into a larger concern or existing perception of business, finance, and corporate behavior. An accusation serves as a narrative device. It is a proxy for a bigger concern. The keywords and key phrases tell us in a plausible and coherent way what happened, who did what to whom, and attach blame. For lack of a better designation, we speak of principal themes becoming crisper and coherent while being found in market-based ties as the *embedding* process.

In the art of shaping an accusation of corporate wrongdoing, the recipe is that it becomes short, simple, and digestible. It has to be sharp, detailed, and tap into some perceived concern. An accusation catches on because there is a fundamental issue that makes intuitive sense to people, so the accusatory message cannot be terribly complex. It takes root because the everyday evidence of wrongdoing betrays the existence of larger concerns about fraud, cheating, duplicity, bribery, and violation of the rules of conduct. At its best, the accusation is framed in the stark terms of good and evil. The market-based socioeconomic tie is the perfect social location or laboratory for the study of this phenomenon.

Historically, there are many focal points of accusations: heresy, witchcraft, ethnocentrism, and discrimination, to mention a few, and, of course, accusations of embezzlement, theft, and deception. Accusations of wrongdoings are ubiquitous social phenomena, full of anger, denunciations, and easily grasped clichés. To quote financial reporters, bribery is a line item (Schubert and Miller 2008), price-fixing a way of life, and false assurances to investors and stockholders can become part of "a systematic campaign…to deceive the investing public" (Wayne 2009). Accusation, allegation, and assertion of wrongdoing are part of public discourse, discourse about alleged corporate crimes and misconduct directed to the world of business, wider societal audiences, public policy, and to state and federal regulators.

Allegations occur in all institutions: in art, science, politics, religion, education, and entertainment, to mention a few. Prescriptive demands are set forth by one class of actors ("the accusers" or "beneficiary actors") that pertain to the behaviors of another class of actors ("the accused" or "target actors"). The accusers "squawk" or complain about behavior of the targets. In the case of markets, it is about socioeconomic wrongdoing. The complaints and allegations of one corporation accusing another corporation of violating the market's prevailing obligations and norms run the gamut from riding roughshod over a contract to lying, cheating, and stealing to betraying an implicit trust to undermining the unwritten agreement to breaking customary ways of doing business. The accusers may be government regulators (Justice Department, Federal Trade Commission, Securities and Exchange Commission, state attorney general), competitors in the same line of business, customers or clients, suppliers, or corporate rating agencies (Standard and Poor's, Moody's) and analysts at investment banks.

Conventional studies of white-collar crime do, of course, bring in the initial accusational dimension indirectly. We argue, however, for explicitly bringing it out by treating detailed allegations as definitions of situations, often deeply institutionalized, that accordingly shape the dual interaction of cultural and social structure. To that end, we discuss the dynamics of the shaping process and the double embeddedness of accusatory action that results. Whereas most criminology and studies of white-collar crime are purportedly aimed at the causes and consequences of illegal acts (Edelhertz 1970; Cressey 2001; Calavita and Pontell 1990), administrative rule violation (Clinard and Yeager 1980), and patterns of conviction (Wheeler and Rothman 1982), this study is less concerned with whether the accused committed a crime and more concerned with the initial accusation – its substantive content, its location in a market relationships, and the frequency of its appearance.

Accusations are about a transgression of the moral order in market behavior. What a corporation, investment house or broker, or state or federal regulator can do is complain about the ploys, disguises, gambits, lies, and even bribes being done by another party. The accuser may complain about the abuse of trust, hint at a solution, invite a response, and seek redress. The offended corporation or business entity may say there is a circumvention of federal and state laws and regulations.

These accusations of misconduct occur when potential "beneficiary actors," or accusers, attempt to enforce their normative demands. They claim a right to make declarations of wrongdoing by the target actors, the accused. The process of accusation is always a two-sided affair. Just as in the sphere of business there is the buyer side and the seller side, and in the status sphere there is the claimant's side and the bestower's side, so too in the moral sphere there is the denouncer and the denounced. The crux of the matter is to explain how accusations as interaction between accuser and accused occur on specific market junctures in the first place. At a later stage in the career of the accusation, agreements can be reached between a company and investigators and lawyers for the Justice Department, for example.

In so-called deferred prosecution agreements, or DPAs, companies acknowledge wrongdoing by not contesting criminal charges, but without formally admitting guilt. Companies avoid criminal prosecution and with most agreements, after two or three years the terms expire with the charges permanently dismissed. While we follow these careers from inception to conclusion, from initial allegation to adamant denial, the interest herein is with the beginning of the process.

The accusation of criminal conduct in business exchange is a long way down a career path of offending behavior. The allegation and charge of criminal behavior or of a white-collar crime occurs after a social actor perceives a behavior as a transgression, points out the condition to others, and tries to convince them that the behavior is a problem. It can be about lying, misstating, misleading, cheating, and stealing. The accusation can be a tool of contestation, a strategic means of communication, and an early indication that some parties to economic exchange in markets are not only dissatisfied about the behavior of their exchange partners, but that they are willing to do something about it.

Our goal is to assess the antecedents of corporate crime and official sanctions – the initial actions of accusation – by bringing together market as culture and market as structure arguments. The responses in a public "cycle of transgressions" (Velho 1976, 268–69) reveal the conditions under which accusations of corporate wrongdoing first appear and whether, when, and under what conditions they continue or not. We can assess the profiles of responses to perceived transgressions: whether the public allegations of market misconduct are (1) single, one-shot events, (2) episodic and cyclical events, or (3) recurrent, repeated, and continuous events.

Accusations of wrongdoing mark the closely monitored frontiers of acceptable socioeconomic conduct. As Erikson (1966) and others following Durkheim have pointed out, the norms themselves are best legitimated by discovering violations and making accusations. Accusations "indicate which abnormalities [meet] with overt disapproval, and for these purposes…it does not matter so much whether these stories were true. It matters more that they were told and retold" (Hopkins 1993, 5). Evidence of the specific telling, and whether it is recurrent or not, is a direct way of understanding the norms and obligations of world of economic exchange. Accusations of wrongdoing by target actors become the focus about an economic actor going at the market in a particular way and someone else − a market exchange partner, stakeholder, stockholder, or regulator − accusing the target of going at it in the wrong way.

The challenge of investigating allegations of misconduct in the market as an institution is determining whether these are one-off episodes to address idiosyncratic wrongs, to express ire, irritation, and anger, or are they are something more patterned, permanent, and public. Newspapers are a common source of information about the occurrence and details of public events. Accusations run the gamut from the highly visible to the routine. For connoisseurs of financial mayhem, and to the delight of business writers and pundits, some of our empirical accusations possess clear-cut villains, details about the alleged business wrongdoing, and plenty of potentially palpable criminal abuses for reformers to correct.

Analyzing allegations of business fraud, bribery, and lying to regulators, for example, is absolutely critical if we are to develop a framework for understanding the dark sides of capitalism; there are challenges associated, however, with these data such as sample selection bias. This is the probability that an accusation against a corporation will not receive any attention in daily newspapers or business press.

Our methodological approach, to be described shortly, casts a wide net with a fine mesh to ensure considerable variation in the occurrence of accusations across all of the corporations analyzed here. Our firms are large, high-capitalization organizations that are closely followed by the press and news media generally. Nevertheless, it is important to note that our analyses rest on the highly newsworthy events such as accusations, allegations, and potentially criminal behavior by visible firms in the capitalist market in the United States.

As one of our informants familiar with white-collar crime put it, "Yes, the accusations can be mundane. There can be instances of *just* finger pointing. Let me use a seasonal analogy. There is 'The Spring,' and there these are green shoots; it *remains to be seen* whether these are annuals or perennials." Case-by-case discussion of accusations in markets describes the annual and perennial finger pointing. Our goal is then to identify general patterns in the data in order to discern some common tendencies in public media accusations. In this Introduction we have tried to outline the main orthodoxies that are entrenched in current scholarship, while pointing out a number of alternative views, some of which seem to us persuasive. A central tenet of our theoretical argument is that market-based transactions and ties (the so-called "pipes of the market") combine with accusations of normative violations (the "prisms of the market") to reveal hot zones of contention.

Accusations have not only cultural but structural manifestations. They become repertoires of wrongdoing when there is a socially and statistically significant co-occurrence of principal themes and market-based ties. This book is about the art of the admixture of culture and social structure as revealed in accusations of economic crime. Repertories are shaped by mixing custom, sentiment, and gossip on one side, with economic exchange relationships and finger pointing on the other. As noted above, the mixing or combining of custom and law is accomplished through four techniques. Again, the four techniques are: honing in on the market-based relationship, stripping the public announcement of its neutral connotations, abbreviating the content of the announcement, and tailoring the recipes with the legal language of fraud, bribery, collusion, and circumvention of official rules and regulations.

Stakeholders, stockholders, boards, and executives use accusations to communicate messages and feelings to insiders and outsiders alike. Finger pointing and allegations of misdirection and complicity strongly co-vary with customers. By this we mean that more red flags are raised on the market-based path involving purchasers of products (i.e., customers and clients including the government as buyer of a firm's products). These are the hot spots in the market. Conversely, publicized warning signs of wrongdoing appear less often on the other side of the market, upstream, with suppliers. We also find accusations of circumvention of formal and administrative rules and regulations, especially collusion and price-fixing. These, of course, involve competitors. As we noted, on this market-based route, industry rivals closely watch and strategically communicate with one another through veiled threats and reactions to what they see as theft, market chicanery, and duplicity.

In their cultural and structural manifestations, accusations are differentially distributed in the market. Companies whose successes depend heavily upon the development and delivery of consumer products (i.e., drugs, cosmetics, food) and the buying, selling, and brokering of investment products and services will be more likely to be accused of deliberate fraud and misrepresentation of those products and services. Companies whose successes depend heavily upon their financial and investment strategies will be more likely to have stronger and broader prohibitions on insider trading and will be more likely to be face accusations of trading on nonpublic, material, proprietary information. Companies whose successes depend on securing large government-related contracts (i.e., military aircraft, commercial aircraft, aerospace) are more likely to be railed against and accused of bribery and extortion. Those whose success depends on public-sector contracts (i.e., infrastructure construction, heavy electrical equipment manufacture, power generation and transmission) are more likely to face public allegations of collusion, bid-rigging, and market allocation. All firms are equally likely to be accused of fraud and misrepresentation of the true financial status of their companies, false filings with the Securities and Exchange Commission, lying to government officials and regulators, along with perjury and obstruction of justice.

Relying on the cultural and structural manifestations of accusations, and studying types of accusations entwined in market-based ties, we hope to disentangle the various types of accusations and their companies in a way that is both theoretically meaningful and offers maximum leverage for revealing, for the first time, the wide range of alleged wrongdoing in capitalism. Importantly, it also reveals occurring repertoires of wrongdoing in the market. This is why public announcements of corporate lying, stealing, and cheating are important in revealing the moral order of society.

2
Red Flags: How to Assemble an Accusation

The red flag is a perspicuous danger-ahead warning. It is a highly charged, often offensive public signal that something is wrong between business partners or between a firm and the government's regulators.

The red flag is in the interstitial spaces between in-group innuendo and slander (gossip) and criminal charges (indictment). The intermediate nature of accusations makes them important for understanding communicative processes and the collective imagination. They contain innuendo as well as the threat of civil or criminal action.

All fraud charges generated by the SEC have criminal counterparts. Whether criminal charges ultimately emerge after the accusations and rebukes is usually a function of intent to defraud; the question is whether the charges can be proved to the far higher criminal standard of beyond a reasonable doubt.

But at the beginning of this process the red flags of rebukes always involve succinct public declarations of what went wrong in a particular economic exchange. They may even give rise to "counter accusations" stating, for example, that the complaints are without factual basis, are exaggerated and stuffed with trumped-up sucker-bait. They always take place within a rich market context full of announcements and their announcers and thus, preserving these words and voices is tantamount to observing the contentious moments in the market.

Variously called "alarm bells," "cautionary flags," and "warning signs," red flags are announcements that "redefine" or "restructure" an ambiguous socioeconomic issue and locate its place in the market. Public allegations are concerted "efforts to find out just what the situation is and what it means" (Turner and Killian 1955, 44; Allport and Postman 1946–47; Creed et al. 2002; Entman 1991; DiFonzo 2008).

But in issuing accusations, the search for information and meaning is laced with anger, disappointment, and feelings of being cheated and lied to. In finding out what it means in the market and in money terms, the publicized "restructuring" is neither fair nor impartial. It assumes guilt rather than innocence. It lays blame. It expresses ire. As an "effort" to define a business situation gone wrong, nuances and caveats are omitted. And there is never anything neutral about a public accusation. Finally, the public accusation of corporate wrongdoing tends to be characterized by a single iconic claim.

In pointing an accusatory finger, the "restructuring" consists of keywords such as "fraud," "pay to play," "embezzlement," "Ponzi scheme," "bribery," or key phrases such as "a breach of fiduciary duties to investors," "conflicts of interest with investment analysts over corporate stock recommendations," "false filing with regulators and securities violations," "engaging in concerted efforts at collusion and market allocation," "using bribery and coercion to maintain a stranglehold on the market," or "systematically using inappropriate accounting procedures."

These keywords, adjectives and phrases accompany descriptions of the company, the behavior of its executives, the market-based tie in which they are embedded, and the history of the events leading up to the alleged wrongdoing. There is a mesh of description and denunciation as phrases and adjectives and adverbs combine to capture the object of judgment as well as the judgment of the object.

Financial losses by investors are not only "ruinous," but also the result of "self-dealing managers" trafficking in "sleazy and underhanded schemes." Accused corporations not only use "questionable business methods" but also "squander" and "loot" as they "run amok."

Relations between corporations and Wall Street analysts are, in several accusation profiles, "incestuous, cozy, and ingrown." Bribery is not only "pay to play" but is portrayed as "the bottom line expense" at several firms and part of the corporate culture – indeed "a way of life in the executive suites."

Collusion and price fixing are viewed as not only "stretching of their rules" but "a supreme heist at the expense of the market's buyers" and a "threat to the welfare of society."

Relationships between corporate executives and investment analysts are not only working agreements but also are part of a "Wall Street–wide culture that routinely issued overly optimistic stock research in order to win investment bank business."

Some more detailed portraits will help show accusations at work and how they are always embedded in market transactions on the one hand, and in definitions and redefinitions of the situation on the other hand. Throughout this example, we see the use of keywords to frame abuses of market-based ties in short, abbreviated, familiar, and easily understood words. We refer to these as market-based ties and principal themes respectively.

In 1985 [MiniScribe]…lost a critical supply contract with IBM, and since sales and inventory were starting to drop…something needed to be done. MiniScribe hired a turnaround specialist, Q. T. Wiles, to help fix things as part of an investment in the company by his venture capital firm, Hambrecht & Quist. Wiles tried reorganizing the company, but instead of improving the company's performance, the new structure just caused chaos.

When that didn't have the desired effect, he decided that MiniScribe should be a 'billion-dollar company,' and pushed the salespeople to get numbers in any way they could. This included things like counting defective drives as good inventory, shipping excess drives to customers and counting them as sales, and counting drives that were still being shipped from the factory in Singapore as stock on hand. One plan that eventually made headlines was executed in late 1987, and was very simple: buy a load of bricks, pack them into boxes, then ship them to a fake customer's warehouse and report them as actual sales to cover the shortfall. (Wikipedia, June 15, 2007)

Creator of a subprime powerhouse that has been touched by crisis. Investigations by attorneys general and banking regulators in more than 30 states had led to suits against Ameriquest and another pillar of the subprime market, the Household International Corporation. The suits were based on consumer complaints and claims of deceptive practices, including loans made with no documentation of a borrower's ability to pay, inflated estimates of house values and the issuing of mortgages with hidden and suddenly escalating adjustable rates. The fortunes of the company…considered the nation's largest subprime mortgage lender, had soared during the long housing

boom as it issued mortgages to people with weak credit histories.
(*New York Times*, March 19, 2008)

A two-year probation from Bristol-Myers Squibb ends today, freeing
the company from federal supervision after a major accounting
scandal and other misconduct... Bristol was accused of exaggerating
revenue by $2 billion from 2002 to 2001 by coaxing wholesalers to
buy far more of its drugs than they could hope to sell... Four of the
company's top executives have been replaced...including the former
chief executive, Peter R. Dolan, who headed Bristol during much
of the time when the irregular accounting took place... Bristol
avoided trial for conspiracy to commit securities fraud by agreeing
in June 2005 to probation under a deferred prosecution agreement
approved by the New Jersey federal prosecutor... (Reuters and the
New York Times, June 15, 2007)

The Securities and Exchange Commission eventually accused Bristol-
Myers Squibb Company of orchestrating a fraudulent earnings
management scheme and deceiving investors about the actual status and
true financial performance of the company. They used deceptive devices
for manipulating accounting reports filed with government regulators.
The company was accused of providing financial incentives to its
wholesalers to purchase pharmaceutical products in advance of demand,
and "inducing" wholesalers to buy excess inventory. They stuffed their
distributor channels with inventory. To do this, they had to "coax" and
bribe wholesalers and distributors.

The stuffing scheme was part of an accounting scandal designed to
inflate the company's sales and earnings figures by sending retailers in the
distribution channel more products than they were able to sell to customers
(dubbed "channel stuffing"). Compaq Computer Corp. joined the long
line of respected electronics and high-tech companies accused, in a loud
barrage of accusations, of using occasionally heavy-handed channeling
practices; counter accusations began to appear as resellers came under heavy
pressure by manufacturers to take on additional, and possibly unwanted,
fake inventory. As noted before in the case of MiniScribe, companies can
employ a clever sleight-of-hand maneuver known as "shipping bricks" to
create the illusion of actual sales and robust financial performance. Instead
of the wink and an envelope inducement and promise of future favors,
MiniScribe covered its sales shortfalls directly through fakery.

Before executives resigned at Bristol-Myers Squibb, before charges of securities fraud were brought, and before a federal prosecutor approved an agreement, federal regulators initially accused Bristol of inflating its earnings. They were accused of establishing a "cookie jar" reserve account and inducing their wholesalers to buy excess inventory. The fraud was conceived as a means to create the appearance of continued strong demand. The business press reported that these accounting gimmicks and "coaxing" gambits were initiated by Bristol's middle-level, regional managers and supported by its top executives. Bristol was under pressure to meet the quarterly earnings estimates of Wall Street securities analysts. Falling short of those targets, Bristol issued materially false and misleading financial statements to federal regulators.

In the case of MiniScribe Corporation, before the formal criminal charges of securities fraud by the Securities and Exchange Commission, investors and creditors accused the company of fraud in connection with the audits of MiniScribe's financial statement in 1987. "The auditors signed off on the financial reports, and the offering was a huge success. That was a decision that the auditors at Coopers & Lybrand (now part of PricewaterhouseCoopers) would regret" (Schilit 2002, 240). The financial reports were bogus, just like the inventory, the fake customer's warehouses, and the make-believe sales figures.

Accusations against MiniScribe morphed into lawsuits for over $1 billion. Coopers & Lybrand eventually settled out of court for $100 million. However, the initial news reports of complaints against MiniScribe and Bristol-Myers Squibb show that before the lawsuits, civil proceedings, criminal indictments, and settlements out of court, there were accusations of market misconduct. Tax regulators, suppliers, and rivals in the business may suspect fakery in sales, bribery, and coaxing as well as other kinds of chicanery. Business competitors may have suspicions of channel stuffing and imaginary inventories. Customers may get irked when the company solicits promises from prospective purchasers to buy more than they want. Company stockholders, investors, and creditors accused the company of financial improprieties. Filing of a bogus financial statement draws the attention of government tax specialists and regulators.

A Wells Notice from lawyers at the Securities and Exchange Commission may have arrived on the desk of Q. T. Wiles at his office at MiniScribe. Peter R. Dolan may have opened his mail to find that he was suspected of stock manipulation and fraud; government investigators will be arriving tomorrow and all company documents must be safeguarded, awaiting the review of authorities. If they find evidence of misconduct, they may initiate further official action. In either case, the notice signals that SEC staff is likely to recommend civil action regarding possible securities violations. A company is told that the commission staff plans to seek approval to begin an investigation. And even before the Wells Notice, a company may file a notice with the commission declaring that it is under investigation by regulatory agencies overseeing markets. Civil suits and criminal suits, along with the filing of injunctions and levy of financial penalties, are only one stage, and a later stage at that, in a continuous and often dramatic public process. From accusation to settlement, the travails of Bristol and MiniScribe were extensively written about in the business press, documented in government filings, and subject to online coverage. Their wrongdoings, from accusation to endpoints, were newsworthy events.

Despite the volume of news reports and apparent drama surrounding the cooking of the books and fraud at MiniScribe and Bristol, and despite the corporate scandals and internal shakeups that followed, we know remarkably little about the careers of accusations, especially the early stages of public announcement of market misconduct. We know more about corporate crime after formal charges are announced: when indictments are handed down, when settlements are reached, and when sentences are pronounced. We know very little about the early initiation of accusations, and even less about their distribution and frequency in economic markets.

We do know that accusations are communicative actions. We know they are public denunciations (Garfinkel 1956). At a minimum they involve a perceived transgression of market behavior or even urge a public hunt for one; and the urging for a hunt can lead to a scandal (Adut 2005). We know little about the publicity and the negative and disruptive effects on the offenders and victims of the accused transgression – parties that include business associates, regulators, rivals, customers, suppliers, professionals, authorities, and audiences.

The literature on market distortion and anticompetitive practices is huge, but empirical studies of the accusation of anticompetition between market participants in business circles are rare. Also rare are sustained efforts to situate the organization of accusations within a model of the larger interorganizational market conduits through which they flow. This is ironic, since accusations are public announcements and a central topic for media's business reports; they are a reliable resource for gossip around the water cooler; and they are a potential resource for demonstrations of resolve (see Adut 2005, 216–21) by government regulators to look into market irregularities and distortions.

Accusations are early-stage warnings of departures from the normative models of market exchange. Someone in a commercial exchange is complaining about something. The trouble is about the business behavior of another. To one party, the other is misleading, misrepresenting, misdirecting, or circumventing the rules. One party signals its suspicion about the market behavior of another. One party shows its mild displeasure by confidentially communicating to the other in private. It is hush-hush and informal. Or an exchange partner spreads a rumor about the offender's market behavior. Or a party takes its complaint up a notch, indicating displeasure by accusing the other of lying, cheating, and/or stealing. This is louder and more formal. A party can go further and harass the other by making public allegations that put the other party under the microscope of the business press; and that may be followed by announcements of pending, more serious, legal action.

Much of the theoretical literature on crime in and around corporations has examined the attributes of individuals, their motives for engaging in illegal behavior, the networks of affiliations in which those individuals are enmeshed, and their opportunities for engaging in wrongful behavior. More recently, scholars have examined the economic and legal conditions that facilitate fraud, deceptive sales practices, favor-trading, price fixing, bribery, and extortion, and the corporation as an organizational weapon – focusing on how people in market exchanges attempt to manipulate transactions by illegal means so as to maximize their interests and short-term goals and to shape market relationships through tools and techniques that violate existing norms and rules. The market presents its economic actors – its sellers, buyers, traders, brokers, professionals, and regulators – with a wide array of competing and conflicting moral values, both legal and illegal.

Sociology analyzes markets in two ways: as structures and as cultural domains. Markets as structures comprise tangible social relations, market roles, role structure, configurations of exchange, supplier and buyer matching, emergent network configurations, and the resulting differential distribution of status and reputation (Baker 1984 and 1990; Faulkner 1983; Baker, Faulkner, and Fisher 1998; Burt 1992, 1993; Leifer 1985; Palmer 1983; Podolney 1993; Swedberg 1994; Tomaskovic-Devey 2007). Markets as cultural domains include the ideas and understandings underlying and guiding economic action. Recipes are reservoirs of knowledge about how to enact market exchange. The socioeconomic literature has such metaphors as "blueprints" that influence supplier and buyer behavior, "rules" that guide competition among rivals, "scripts" that underlie commercial transactions, and "frames" that pattern the exchange of goods and services (Abolafia 1997; Carruthers and Espeland 1991; DiMaggio 1994; Fligstein 1996; Swedberg 2003, Chapters IX, X; Zelizer 1988).

Recipes serve as reservoirs of ideas about how to conduct market interaction. When a market actor selects a recipe, it affects economic behavior in four ways: (1) by identifying a nexus of exchange in a market as an opportunity set (a structural and contextual feature), (2) by influencing how social actors define opportunism and illegality as interests (a cultural and constitutive feature), (3) by constraining their efforts on their own behalf (a cultural and regulatory feature), and (4) by shaping the market actor's capacity to enact interests and its goals (a structural and cultural feature). The structural conduits for exchange with the cultural content of exchange are a rapprochement between the two approaches. Finally, an empirical focus on white-collar illegality (Shapiro 1980), crime content and its criminals (Shapiro 1990), exchange logics of exploitation (Best and Luckenbill 1982), opportunism in transactions (Williamson 1975), and rent extraction (McChesney 1997) revives interest in the sociological study of illegal behavior in markets.

Certain features shape wrongdoing in an organizational field. Markets as cultures are constituted by cultural symbols and practices from which actors compose, select, and enact forms of misconduct. The composition of interest is a reservoir of potential ideas, frames, blueprints, and schemas for wrongdoing. Social actors in the economy may incorporate these scripts and schemas into their array of behavioral possibilities. They may select from this array for possible use in and around situations of economic exchange (e.g., buyer and seller, principal and agent, professional and client).

The array may be extensive, or a long "list," of possibilities; the array may be restrictive, or a shorter list of possibilities. Each idea on the long or short list has room for maneuvering. The maneuvering room or space may be wide, which would allow the actors plenty of latitude in implementing the item on the list. The maneuvering space may be narrow, in which case the actors are highly constrained in what they can do in expanding a single recipe idea into a practice or routine. When we speak of highly scripted social behaviors, we implicitly imagine a short list with narrow latitude.

So what is the relationship between recipes and routines, ideas and actions? Ideas shape choices or selections and become real when acted on, becoming the routines we call lying, cheating, stealing, and betraying. But that is not all. There are also ideas and understandings of social roles and which positions are preferred as the locus of exchange. The question here is how and to what extent the positions of influence and authority in the illegal exchange are related to, and supported by, the power, rank, and responsibility of formal and legal roles in the focal organization. Who are the role actors on both sides of the exchange? In a corporate exchange conduit, for example, sellers and buyers are roles actors with positions in their respective organizations. What are their formal rank and roles? Are top- or middle-level executives involved from the corporate side? Are top-level, middle- or lower-level personnel involved from the other side of the exchange? Is the exchange between a top-level marketing manager and a purchasing agent, the chief financial officer and an investment banking analyst, the chief executive officer and a nation–state official? In other words, what is the structure of the exchange partners as a combination of role occupants? The triad of recipe, routine, and role constitutes the enactment process.

Social actors learn about, think about, choose, and enact strategies of misconduct in different social contexts. The market roles and network location of social actors are the tangible conduits through which flow the content of illegal (and legal) action. The social context for conduit and content is constituted by, but not limited to, the information the parties have of one another, or the awareness contexts in which interaction takes place (Glazer and Strauss 1965), the shared knowledge about techniques for expropriation of valued resources (Edelhertz 1970; Shapiro 1980; Simon and Hagan 1999; Geis and Meier 1977), the known tools for deliberate creation and organization of ignorance (Erickson 1990), the current vocabularies for explanation and justification (Tilly 2006), the scripts for secrecy, successful models of coverup (Katz 1977), and ways of making visible the processes of trust and trust violation (Gambetta 1990; Fukuyama 1995). Markets as structure and markets as culture are often contrasted. The argument and examples to follow show the logic of improper dealings in market exchanges (the culture of markets) intertwined with market roles (the structure of markets).

Illegal actions such as extorting kickbacks from companies seeking state business, fraudulently misleading companies seeking to either supply or buy from an exchange partner, and extortion are amongst the examples. These actions are highly scripted with tightly framed rules and may include boycotts, threats, hostage taking, and ransom. Extortion is a classic form of antagonistic cooperation: the target knows what actions are available and the extortionist dictates his preferences. If the hostage is a person, extortion is kidnapping. If the hostage is a victim's reputation, the extortion is blackmail. If the hostage is a business contract, extortion is racketeering.

Fraud, on the other hand, rests on deliberately created ignorance, misrepresentation, closed awareness, and deception. Favor trading, bribery, and kickback rest on conflicts of interest, misdirection, and open awareness between the parties. Collusion, structurally located in the competitive relations among industry peers, is cooperative antagonism among rivals and involves promises, mutual assurances, game playing, and prisoner dilemma tradeoffs. This scraping away of the brighter surfaces of markets as presented in the organizational strategy literature throws light on the "shortcuts to success" (Hirsch and Pozner 2006) taken by large corporations.

Fraud and economic misconduct appear in various guises. Individual appliance repairmen defraud individual consumers when they overcharge for parts, charge for but fail to install new parts, or misrepresent the age and condition of used replacement parts (Vaughan and Carol 1975). This may be analyzed as a case of single fraud, or as multiple frauds on multiple targets. Prudential Corporation intentionally misrepresented material facts about its oil and gas partnerships: top analysts deliberately inflated the assets of the firm, and securities analysts issued buy recommendations to their potential investors on the basis of those false financial statements (Eichenwald 1995; Sharp 1995; Elliot and Schroth 2002). General Electric and other electrical equipment manufacturers defrauded public and private utility companies by fixing prices in the famous electrical equipment price-fixing conspiracy (Baker and Faulkner 1993; Smith 1961). Their collusion caused publicly owned utilities to needlessly pay higher prices for steam turbines (buyers and state actors), distorted the consensus forecast of corporate earnings by analysts (investment banks), and warped the purchasing behavior of corporate investors in the stock market (buyers).

In market sectors, repertoires of wrongdoing change. In one of the earliest and most thorough treatments of corporate violations of administrative rules and regulations, Clinard and Yeager's (1980) work shows that investigations of wrongdoing and administrative inquiries are rife in some industries and rare in others. At the top of their mid-1970s list are oil, autos, and pharmaceuticals. Fifteen years later, that list has changed. At the top of our 1985–2005 list of accused are securities and investment firms, financial companies, and corporations in the computer and electronic equipment industry, followed by oil, autos, and pharmaceuticals.

3
Fighting Words and Key Phrases

Every public accusation is shaped. It has some literary form, which is to say it is written in some style. Most of them, by design, convey one fairly simple idea: they preserve the particulars of their corporate wrongdoers while bringing them into conformity with a general type of wrongdoing. The red flag, for example, is a fusion of form and content so that we can discern what it means by examining not only what it says but how it says it.

Accusations are best served up through articles and aperçus. We throw a wide net over corporations using following sources: (1) LexisNexis and Dow Jones Interactive corporate data archives; (2) stories, editorials and commentary in the *Wall Street Journal*, the *New York Times*, the *Los Angeles Times*, *San Jose Mercury News*, *Financial Times*, and the *Washington Post*; (3) articles, editorials, and commentary in magazines such as *Fortune*, *Forbes*, *BusinessWeek*, the *New Yorker*, *Vanity Fair*, *Rolling Stone*; (4) Edgar Archives and regulatory filings with the Securities and Exchange Commission, especially the Wells Notices of potential civil action by the SEC (a Wells Notice is issued to a target of an investigation to give the company and its executives an opportunity to provide facts or testimony to regulators to convince them that the filing of a wrongdoing complaint is unwarranted); and finally, (5) Internet sites specializing in white-collar crime filings under the False Claims Act. (The False Claims Act allows private citizens and former employees of corporations to sue companies they believe to be cheating the government. The act was originally passed to fight profiteering during the Civil War. In recent years it has been used to bring allegations of Medicare fraud.)

Our choice of newspapers as a primary data source is based on the central role of the general and business press in "shaping the attention of audiences" (Warner and Molotch 1993; Jonsson, Greve, and Fujiwara-Greve 2009). By tracking an accusation story, annotating the narrative, we follow the moral career of the keywords and catchphrases. The keywords and catchphrases are attached to the corporation, but our primary unit of observation and analysis is the public allegation and how it is linked in and linked with a market-based tie. Thus, we first find the initial accusation. Then we construct a running record on it, looking for further public announcements, reactions, commentary, and editorials. We also keep a running record of the placement of the story in the newspaper: its location, length, official sources, level of seriousness, and degree of magazine-style story production (see Klineberg 2002, Chapter 5; Tuchman 1973).

Financier Bernard Madoff was indicted and charged with orchestrating fraud through his eponymous financial firm. This is an exemplary high-profile case that began as a series of allegations that were then verified and then taken seriously (see Klinenberg 2002, 202). It is also an example of our data collection strategy wherein we would follow the story from initial announcements in the *New York Times* and the *Wall Street Journal* to editorials and articles in these newspapers as well as articles in *BusinessWeek*, the *Washington Post*, and one in *Vanity Fair* titled "Bernie Madoff's Private World: the money, the madness, and the mysteries" (Seal 2009).

We would continue to follow the story and keep a record of whether or not regulators in Washington, for example, get involved, open a case file, and expand their investigation. Firms and commissioners report when the Securities and Exchange Commission's enforcement division upgrades its informal inquiry to a formal investigation, a key turning point in the career of the accusation and, of course, a key turning point in the moral career of the accused corporation and its executives. Upgrades give regulators the power to issue subpoenas. Upgrades and the widening of corporate scandal are followed by the business press and allow us to track the timing of subsequent events such as the firing of executives, managers, and officials, realignment of board members and their responsibilities, the progress of internal corporate investigations, recording of additional charges for taxes, announcements of changes of previous financial statements, and the possibility of further criminal or civil sanctions against the company or certain individuals.

In sociology, examination of qualitative statements concerning allegations and content-based coding of accusations is interpretive and requires considerable judgment (Porac, Wade, and Pollock 1999; Wade, Porac, and Pollock, 1997; Krippendorff 1980, 62–63; Weber 1985; Holsti 1969). Finding detailed evidence of the episode of wrongdoing and accurately coding the location of the accusation in economic exchange paths is a formidable but tractable research operation. The amended quarterly (10-Q/A) and annual (10-K-A) financial statements with the SEC contain a wealth of detailed information on the status of a company, its executives, and whether a firm is subject of various actions by federal and state regulators. The SEC filings inevitably provoke numerous press reports, journalistic essays, and reactions of investors, regulators, and business pundits.

The tracking of keywords, key phrases and the corporations involved in LexisNexis (on the *New York Times, Wall Street Journal, Washington Post*) provides timely information on what happened as well as what journalists and analysts make of what happened, including the common categories, affective catchphrases, and feelings that are used to characterize wrongdoing by companies, executives, and even by sectors of the economy (financial industry, analysts, rating agencies, regulators). News reports often quote experts on corporate governance and Wall Street analysts who follow the industry in which the accused works.

We follow content analytic protocols used in the studies of social movements and in the communication studies literature (Gamson 1992; Creed et al. 2002; Entman 1991; Ghaziani and Ventresca 2005). Our focus is on accurately classifying and coding accusations by asking two questions after reading each article and its abstract: (1) what core concept(s) unify the central allegations in the brief? (2) What market-based ties are the parties involved in? We used a technique similar to that used by Porac, Wade, and Pollock (1999), and Wade, Porac, and Pollock (1997) to develop a content-analysis protocol for coding the object of the judgment and the judgment of the object: the market-based tie and the principal theme.

We start by identifying the concepts we want to analyze (i.e., fraud, collusion, bribery, obstruction of justice, etc.) and, in an iterative manner, develop a content-analysis coding scheme and code book of key words and key terms that pair the *co-occurrence* of market tie with principal theme. Throughout, we use Turner and Surace's strategy for coding symbols, especially in documenting how symbols are shaped in problematic situations. We found that symbols of accusation become shorter, sharper, more concise, and stripped of their "alternative connotations" (Turner and

Surace 1975, 125–27) as the principal theme and market-based tie unfold together over time. Our emergent hypothesis was this: the alignment of accusation theme and market-based tie occurs more frequently when the key words, phrases, and verbs "come to evoke unambiguously unfavorable feelings" (Turner and Surace 1975, 125; compare with McLean 1998).

It is of critical importance in the conceptualization and coding of accusations of corporate crime to distinguish between crimes by the corporation and crimes against the corporation. Our working definition of organizational wrongdoing or misconduct was "violation of laws, regulations, or rules by acts of omission or commission by individuals or groups of individuals acting in their organizational roles in behalf of organizations" (Vaughan 1996, 102). Collusion involving industry peers or rivals for the furtherance of organization goals is an example of crimes by corporations. There are, for example, 157 cases of colluding in our dataset (see Table 2). On the other hand, crimes against corporations resemble Edwin Sutherland's original definition of white-collar crime as "a crime committed by a person of respectability and high social status in the course of his occupation." Of particular interest for our purpose is the accusation of "violations of the law committed in the course of a legitimate occupation or financial pursuit by persons who hold respected positions in their communities" (Coleman 1987, 407), where those persons hold trusted positions in large corporations and use those positions for personal rather than organizational gain. Using material, proprietary, and confidential information to trade on corporate stocks for personal gain is an example of circumvention of government rules and regulations, an accusation of a crime against the corporation. There are 127 cases of insider trading (see Table 2). There are 110 cases of accusations of embezzlement and looting firms for personal gain, clear allegations of crimes against the corporation.

We acknowledge that accusations of crimes against firms – such as embezzlement – may result in an undercount of cases due to the fact that these infractions of corporate rules may be handled confidentially and quietly, never resulting in public accusations of wrongdoing. Corporations that find employees who have violated company policy have a tendency to fire the violator without suing the person or airing the alleged violation in the press or before public agencies (Skolnick 1980, 250–52). One of our corporate informants reminded us of a story he read in the *Wall Street Journal* concerning an accountant who had held jobs at several, large corporations. He had embezzled funds from all of them. When the embezzlements were discovered, each firm fired the violator; however, none accused him in public nor sued him. In fact, each firm gave him positive recommendations for a job at another company. The point is that monitoring and enforcing insider trading prohibitions and rules governing looting and embezzlement, and even bribery internal to the firm, can be handled in ways that do not result in public allegations of crimes against the firm.

A socially and statistically significant portion of the art of the accusation is to shape "community feeling" towards the wrongdoing (capital "crime" and wrongdoing) and the target of the wrongdoer (a specific economic role as target, i.e., customer, supplier, regulator, etc.). We call this the "shaping" of the accusation and the effect or "feeling it evokes" in the market. "Whether the mass media passively reflect community sentiment or whether they actively mold it, or whether, as we suppose, some combination of the two processes occurs, we should still be justified in using the content of mass media to indicate community feeling (Turner and Surace 1975, 125). In our coding we follow Ragin (1994) and use a "retroductive" coding scheme that alternates between a priori and inductive coding of the corporate cases and their accusation types. For at least three reasons, the public accusation can reveal the sentiment behind economic action that is considered illegitimate: such economic action is (1) fundamentally *inconsistent* with deeply institutionalized norms and values in the market, (2) widely viewed as a *threat* to the perpetuation of these norms, and (3) vehemently *denounced* by significant actors (customers, suppliers, regulators) in the market.

A scandal at a manufacturing company, a widening investigation by the SEC's enforcement division, and an upgrade from informal inquiry to formal investigation brought forth the following comment by a professor who raised questions about how companies like the accused do business: "It is hard to believe that something on this scale could be so organized," the professor said, "and that no control was in place to catch it. It shows a deficit." This story line is followed by the comments of an analyst who said, "The corruption affair overshadowed everything. The board has a great burden of responsibility to quickly find a successor in the foreseeable future." The analyst then noted that the firm's stock price had not suffered. "The company has identified [millions] in suspicious payments over a seven-year period at a division that makes telecommunications equipment. Those payments may have been used as bribes to foreign officials to win contracts." The analyst continued, "[The company] said it would expand its search for similar payments to other divisions and begin looking at payments that might have been made in cash."

Another example of an accusation sequence concerns major investment and commercial banks. Investment banks underwrite securities and commercial banks accept deposits and make loans. The repeal of the Glass–Steagall Act of 1933 occurred in the late 1990s and ushered in an era of consolidation and integration within the financial services industry, with mixed results in legal and illegal spheres. Citigroup bankers and analysts found themselves accused of being at the center of some of the biggest corporate scandals of the time, including the collapse of Enron and WorldCom and investigations into Wall Street research tainted by conflict of interest. Excerpts from the files on Citigroup and Bausch & Lomb reveal the intermixture of standard content characteristics (who, when, with what effect (Holsti 1968, 622–44)) with labels of the events as "scandals."

A journalist writes about the bank's attempt to reorganize its management, slim its "bulging" corporate compliance rank, rein in its operating budget, streamline its managerial chain of command, and enhance its competitiveness. "Citigroup, like other banks," the journalist asserts, "was tarred by its dealings with Enron and WorldCom and by investigations into analysts' conflicts during the Internet boom. A series of rapid, huge Eurobond trades by Citigroup bankers, referred to as a 'Dr. Evil' trading strategy, roiled markets in Europe in August 2004. That fall, Citigroup's private bank had a run-in with Japanese regulators over lax money-laundering controls. For more than a year, Citigroup was banned by the Federal Reserve from making a big acquisition until its financial house was in order" (Dash 2007). Intra-firm content (of Citigroup) reveals the contents of earlier SEC filings, sketches of the government charges, and the internal investigation that followed.

In another series of news reports on Bausch & Lomb, the best-known contact lens maker was portrayed as a business with a "tarnished" brand name and image. Poor management, excessive pay packages for its executives, and mediocre performance led to the firm being placed on the auction block. Speaking about the chief executive officer, the front page article of the Sunday business section of the *New York Times* said the following: "Even as the big picture at his company became blurred – by such things as accounting scandals that delayed public filings for years, a devastating recall of its flagship lens solution and a 90 percent drop in earnings from 2004 to 2006 – legal minutiae in his contract guaranteed him an outsize pay package." In October 2005 the company disclosed an internal inquiry into its troubling accounting practices, and by December government investigations reached into its Asian business and its financial reporting. In late 2005 the story continues; the firm said there was "material weakness in its controls over financial reporting" and in early 2007 it restated earnings for the first four years of the chief executive's tenure at Bausch. In 2006 the federal government started tracking cases of infections caused by its lens solution products, led by its ReNu line. The company was "sharply and publicly criticized" by the Food and Drug Administration for "not alerting health officials more quickly about the Singapore outbreak and for numerous manufacturing deficiencies at the plant where Bausch produced ReNu." This criticism was used to accuse the firm of consumer fraud, and more than four hundred lawsuits from consumers claim that their vision had been permanently harmed. An investment analyst summed up the scandal of troubled operations, false filing, and damaged brand name by noting that while Bausch had experienced problems before, the trouble this time around "is that in the past, there was a management problem but the brand was intact. Today, they also have a problem managing the business but the brand name is tarnished. And that's a much bigger challenge" (Schwartz 2007).

The exchange path between a manufacturer and its purchasers, for example, involves a high volume of accusations of fraud compared to other paths. This suggests exchange ties provide conduits for the exchange of goods and services as well as paths for transmitting expectations about prices and profits, rules, and routines. But these exchange ties are not simply conduits for economic exchange, but are also potential paths for allegations and accusations of business misconduct, encompassing lying, looting, and bribery, for example. The exchange paths in markets contain not only control projects of interface negotiation, but more nefarious projects as well – projects of opportunism and illegal misdeeds in profit and price behavior.

The corporation's economic links to other organizations is a network of suppliers, customers and buyers, investment analysts, corporate rating agencies, and federal and state regulators. The socioeconomic exchange routes are the following: (1) the focal organization or business as a central player – the hub in the social field; (2) organizations that produce similar products and services, that is, competitors, peers, or rivals; (3) organizations that supply material, financial, symbolic, and technical products and services – lawyers, lobbyists, advertising agencies, accounting firms, and capital (retail banks); (4) organizations that purchase, use, or distribute the products or services – clients, customers, purchasers, wholesalers, and retailers; (5) investment banks, brokerage firms, securities analysts, financial columnists, investor services; and (6) state organizations that license, regulate, and have jurisdiction over the focal organization or business – regulatory agencies, investigative panels, internal bureaus, enforcement bodies, and federal prosecutors.

These market-based ties constitute a societal sector (Scott and Meyer 1978) or organizational field of social actors (DiMaggio 1991). There is the market's tie location and content, the accused, the accusation, and the story line through which the keywords are arranged into a meaningful narrative (Czarniawska-Joerges 1997). Are accusations differentially distributed on the exchange paths in the market? Which accusations appear on which routes, and with what frequency? Where do the "hot spots" occur in the market? Where do the more vitriolic and negative allegations appear? Which accusations and their target corporations garner attention on a wide scale and become "celebrity problems" or business scandals?

Honesty and trust are essential ingredients for market exchange and conformity to industry norms. The violations of honesty and trust can seem perfectly clear with the benefit of hindsight; deception, however, is notoriously difficult to spot, and unfolds over time. A business rival, supplier, or customer complains to a regulator (Shapiro 1984, 44–68). Regulators look into the matter. Then the potentially offending firm and its executives receive notice. The notice may come as a grand jury subpoena. The US Attorney's Office makes a request for documents related to the firm's business dealings. The FBI announces that it is conducting a potential fraud investigation. Or the company says in a filing with the Securities and Exchange Commission that a subpoena has arrived. The company says it is cooperating with the investigation. More serious still, a couple of top echelon executives are found liable for violations of securities fraud by making false statements to accountants. This results in formal complaints to the authorities; when the authorities do something about them and initiate an investigation, the corporate actor and its executive personnel move into the social category of the newsworthy.

Newsworthy investigations provide the data for an analysis of the sequence outlined above, and for establishing the frequencies of accusations in market-based ties, which tell us, in turn, via the specifics of accusations, what the operating rules everyone has routinely accepted for that link are. When an accusation appears in the press, the public stage of the accusation's career begins. Several other steps follow the public accusation, reflecting the concern of executives over the tarnishing of personal and corporate reputations. First, the media sharpen or condense the story, interpreting it by assimilating it into one of a few standard scenarios, which put blame in one place or another. Second, this keeps it in the public eye, producing outrage and provoking damage control by executives. Third, the keywords of the standard stories (whose definition will be part of our analysis) are variations on the theme of executives breaking promises due to their self-interest and greed.

The consternation, outrage, and damage control following initial accusations are serious matters for the tarnished corporate actor and its executives. So too are the entertainment values that attend the never-too-distant specter of adversity. There is nothing like a potentially long and loud scandal to activate the media. In addition to market repertoires and their career, the print media and television participate in the narrative plot of the wrongdoing. "The media do not simply provide information about events, they also tell stories that seek to engage their audience and increase their desire for more information on the subject of the story" (Rindova et al. 2006, 56). And vitriolic exaggeration also appears in the quotations from the accusers. For example, a microcomputer and telecommunications equipment maker is not only accused of misrepresenting the status and availability of equipment during the procurement process, but also of misleading official by "repackaging the products of another company and demonstrating an information-coding device that was 'nothing more than an empty box with blinking lights'" (Pear 1985). The Challenger rocket boosters manufactured by Morton Thiokol Inc. were not only sold to NASA through the use of "false and fraudulent claims," but the National Aeronautics and Space Administration conspired "to give false testimony to mislead investigators" in the aftermath of the space shuttle disaster (Boffey 1986).

The portrayal of what happened can take time to unfold. In the world of government-backed mortgages, for several years Freddie Mac smoothed out the recognition of losses, and this procedure raised few objections. "Until 2004, Freddie used a set of rules known as 'hedge accounting' to recognize gains or losses on such derivatives over many years rather than including them immediately in earnings" (Hagerty and Perez 2009). Accusations of accounting irregularities forced Freddie in

2003 to "reexamine" many of its accounting policies after regulators and auditors found that the giant mortgage company had violated rules in an attempt to "smooth out" earnings. In 2008 a confidential report by the investigative firm Kroll concluded that "inappropriate application" of accounting rules "enabled Freddie to defer billions of dollars of losses incurred from 2001 through 2004."

In some cases, the portrayal of an accusation and its principal theme takes time to emerge; in other cases, the theme and the market-based tie are clearly defined in the initial announcement. Both emergent and immediate, they reveal a wealth of new empirical regularities about what is made of the reported accusation and its content. Data transformation of these occurrences constitutes a running record (Webb 1966, 75–87). This record can discover misdeeds and narratives of them, a record of "what happened" and "that which is said to have happened" (see Trouillot 1995 in Walton 2001, xiv). The evidence on accusations is on 1,963 companies with market valuation of $50 million and more that are publicly traded on the New York and American stock exchanges – manufacturing firms, utilities, insurance companies, and investment firms. These are called large-capitalization firms. It is straightforward to know quite accurately what an enterprise is worth in the market. So if, for instance, an oil company has 20 million shares selling at $20 a share, its market capitalization is $400 million. From a sample of 427 so-called "high cap" companies, or 21 percent, from 1985 to 2006, a record is compiled of the accused firms and the nature of the accusations. We also compiled information on the accusers – another firm, such as a rival, supplier, customer, or a government agency such as the Justice Department, Securities and Exchange Commission, the US Attorney General, and so on.

The 1985 Compustat data file provides detailed financial information about each company (for details of this information in an earlier report, see Baker, Faulkner, Fisher 1998, 162). The triad of accusation, accused, and accuser is structural in that it is located on a market route or exchange conduit for economic exchange. The triad is cultural because the principal theme of wrongdoing is a cultural motif loaded with cultural content about lying, cheating, stealing, and impeding or impairing the behavior of market-based exchange partners. The examples to follow are drawn from a file of the count and content of accusations to appear in national newspapers, business magazines, and on-line sources from December 1994 to February 2006.

Qualitative informant interviews were conducted with a dozen corporate accountants and consultants and a director of a division of securities (Faulkner 2009), and for our initial fraud and embezzlement case, we informally interviewed investigators from the district attorney's office, the court-appointed receiver, the forensic accountant for the Ventura County district attorney's case, and a sample of investors as respondent interviewees (see Baker and Faulkner 2004).

For the quantitative analysis, the sample firms are large-capitalization businesses such as Abbott Labs, Atlantic Richfield, American Airlines Inc., Bausch & Lomb, Boeing Co., Bristol-Meyers Co., Chevron Corp., Citigroup, Coca-Cola Co., Dow Chemical, Disney, Exxon, Halliburton Co., Johnson & Johnson, Pfizer Inc., MiniScribe, Mobile Corp., Union Carbide Corp., Upjohn Co., and Xerox Corp. Mergers and buyouts have changed the ownership of some of the companies; those that continue to file their own financial documents remain eligible our on list. Companies are assigned to a standard industrial classification group according to the business that contributed most to their sales. We also track the changing names of firms that occur under various circumstances (leverage buyout, merger, acquisition, etc.) and retain the original name to appear in the temporal data set (i.e., Libbey-Owens-Ford became Trinova Corp. and in our list of firms and their accusations it is called Libbey-Owens-Ford rather than Trinova Corp.). We focus on 1,103 accusations of economic wrongdoing by corporations from the fourth quarter of 1994 to the first quarter of 2006 (Appendix B lists the companies and the number of their accusations over this period of time; then look to Table 2 for the distribution of accusations by their recipes and routes).

Publicized accusations of wrongdoing vary in their number, their market location, and their keyword descriptors. Table 1 presents an array of accusations from informal gossip and innuendo, through quiet management of rule breaking and deviance, through public accusations to formal, and announced, indictments and criminal/civil charge. The following three paragraphs include examples of the interstitial nature of public accusations, standing between informal gossip and formal indictment:

Regulators announce in a press conference, evidence of wide-scale accounting improprieties by top executives in advance of their being awarded hefty yearly pay packages and bonuses. Antitrust authorities are suspicious of two dominant firms in the auction market and open an inquiry into a conspiracy to lower sellers' commissions. Justice Department authorities are suspicious of attempts to raise prices and allocate bids to customers in the lysine cartel. Regulators announce their request for documents from investment banks, because they suspect illegal reciprocal arrangements in the bank's awarding of initial public offerings (IPOs) to their valued corporate clients – misdeeds involving reciprocal and illegal dealing by parties undermining investor confidence in the market.

In the software business, and in the soft drink industry, a firm sues its competitive rival for stealing its proprietary products and information, alleged misconduct by an industry peer. In the world of student financial aid and exchange between borrowers and lenders, some colleges and universities are suspected of steering students to loan companies. The loan companies then kick money back to the colleges in accordance with the volume of business generated by these students, as well as in return for preferential placement on lender lists. These loan companies are engaged in deceptive business practices, inherent conflicts of interest, illegal steering, and bribery.

Federal prosecutors disclose that they suspect improper payments and transactions over seven years – many of them involving bribery and kickback schemes – in the German, Switzerland, and Italian international telecommunications industry, mutual misdeeds by corporations, customers, and governments. The California attorney general's office charges a large medical firm with bribery and criminal misconduct in its dealings with professional clients. The San Diego office announces a sweeping criminal investigation into suspected bribery and influence peddling between a major aerospace contractors and a member of Congress. The Manhattan district attorney's office indicts a major political figure in Brazil involved in a construction kickback scheme, at the expense of taxpayers, involving money laundering through commercial and investment banks; and the office of the inspector general begins an investigation into the bungling of offshore oil and gas leases by the Interior Department along with accusations of lying by the department's secretary to a Senate panel.

This book began with an interest in the business press and its coverage of markets and misconduct. Max Weber called for a large-scale effort to examine the role of the press in society (see Krippendorff 1980, 13). The press is important in reporting on industries and markets. The press is also important in reporting on accusations of wrongdoing. These reports of events can affect the reputation of market actors. The emphasis is first placed on the accusations; on the alleged wrongdoings rather than the putative wrongdoers; on the crimes, not the criminals (see Shapiro 1990). The allegations and their actors portrayed here are illustrative rather than exhaustive.

The literature on high-profile organizational scandals of economic fraud, executive embezzlement, insider trading, bribery, kickbacks, and obstruction of justice is vast. Invariably, one reads about contending executives, boards, shareholders, legislative committees, suppliers, buyers, regulators, prosecutors, defense lawyers, members of Congress, and those in the executive branch of government.

Allegations of wrongdoing cannot be understood except in certain contexts. The context of exchange, the way recipes are turned into practices, the "contested" allegations of wrongdoing by those in a position to say something about and do something about the behavior, and then the possible legal outcomes must all be taken into consideration. That market features shape ideas into action does not argue that these features operate in isolation from one another.

The path leading to accusations of wrongdoing depends on many things. Accusations are dependent, or contingent, on events that precede them (Becker 1998, 32–35; Velho 1976). The contingencies shaping accusations of wrongdoing are a "network of people whose cooperative activity…produces the kinds of [illegal] works that a [market] world is noted for" (Becker 1982, x). Such cooperative networks as structures exist in markets endowed with mechanisms that promote connection between exchange partners, potential opportunities for wrongdoing, and steps in the process of how improper dealings in and around participants become possible (Becker 1998, 60–63). Every market-based tie between a corporation and the outside is simultaneously a link of cooperation and getting things done for mutual benefit, and a possible location for the accusations and perpetuation of various kinds of illegality.

Inside the company, for example, allegations can fly back and forth between directors and executives, between executives and their managers, managers and their staffs. Keeping these under wraps is obviously critical for the firm's reputation and status. Stealing information and then trading on it is one recipe of misconduct; lying and misrepresentation of the firm's products is another. There are allegations of crimes against the company by wayward or rogue employees and executives. There are accusations of crimes by the firm directed toward its interorganizational market partners: customers complain, suppliers squawk, analysts argue, and rivals revolt. They "go public" with an accusation of misconduct. Customers, for instance, do not like their prices, think they are getting gouged; they may see seller collusion and file a complaint with federal, state, or local regulators.

Rivals, for their part, get fed up with finding infringement on their patents, depriving their earlier innovations of their value or utility. Companies see sales and marketing forces as "going too far" or "pushing too fast" on a peer's traditional market share. In the first case, they accuse the firm of wrongdoing and file a patent lawsuit. In the second, they file a civil antitrust suit against a competitor. Accusations of collusion are frequently transmitted along exchange routes in telecommunications, biotechnology, semiconductors, liquor (especially the beer business), soft drinks, and aerospace industries. Accusations of insider trading are enmeshed along paths in investment banking, brokering, and hedge funds.

This raises the possibility that certain exchange paths may include cultural niches for accusations (and their accusers) that specialize in the transmission of basic market norms about proper business conduct. The recipes and routines are neither casually transmitted nor randomly distributed in markets. Repertoires are patterned and being patterned, they reveal the inner workings of markets as normative cultures. Some exchange routes are robust, with relatively high percentages of accusations. When the recipes of misrepresentation, misdirection, and circumvention are enacted on exchange routes, they are valuable repertoires of information about market conduct, about what is and is not permissible, and about where the "bright line" boundaries of proper (and improper) behavior are etched. The participants enact accusations. They alert other specific market participants that their business behavior can be, and is, of concern.

As noted earlier, accusations are abbreviated, focused, and easily digestible signs of discontent. They are often a symbol of a long-simmering resentment between exchange partners. They are vehement denunciations by market actors. They follow a direct path to the culprit. They also seek to draw stark distinctions between good and evil. And when they achieve their effect, they focus unwanted attention and negative publicity on the accused.

4
Market Exchanges Gone Sour: Six Fields of Action

Every line between a corporation and the outside is simultaneously a link of cooperation and getting things done for mutual benefit and a possible location for accusations and perpetration of various kinds of illegality. This lets us ask several questions: How are accusation stories, enacted through stripping, leveling, and attributing, distributed along market-based lines? Which accusations appear on which market routes with a high degree of frequency?

Several steps follow the public accusation, reflecting the concern of executives over the tarnishing of personal corporate reputations. First, the media enlarge the story, interpreting it by assimilating it to one of a few standard scenarios, which puts blame in one place or another. Second, this keeps it in the public eye, producing outrage and provoking damage control by executives. Third, the standard stories (whose elaboration will be part of our description and analysis) all tend to stick to one of a handful of templates and are variations on the theme of executives breaking promises due to their self-interest, self-dealing, and greed on the one hand, and their need to protect, defend, and justify the actions of their corporation on the other.

Market-Based Tie Number 1: Accusations of Wrongdoing In and Around the Corporation

Many intermediate accusations originate in formal and complex organizations. These may include abuses of power, abuse of trust, and business misconduct (Wheeler and Rothman 1982; Vaughan 1999, 287). The study of corporate crime focuses on employees using the firm as a resource for transforming recipes of deception and disguise into routines of wrongdoing. Employees may exploit their positions of trust, their access to information, and their network connections. In addition, business organizations can provide normative support for wrongdoing, the means for carrying out misconduct, the devices for concealing it from other insiders in the firm, and techniques for covering it over so that outsiders, such as federal and state investigators, cannot detect the potentially illegal practices and routines.

There is a cognitive recipe for misrepresentation and deception. Embezzlement via misappropriation of assets is the classic way scholars think about the "privatization" of lying, cheating, and stealing. In the solo version, the lone employee steals corporate funds for personal gain without the knowledge or consent of others (Cressey 1953; Seidler, Andrews, and Epstein 1977). In the coordinated version, dubbed "collective embezzlement," several employees conspire to expropriate corporate capital, conceal their actions, and bribe coworkers in the event they uncover the wrongdoing. Moving up the chain of command, we start with employees stealing from employers; then at the next level up, executives stealing from the owners; managers stealing from stockholders; board members stealing from stakeholders.

As a result of stepped-up enforcement of insider-trading and bribery laws, corporations can reevaluate their practices, hire consultants to help them ferret out possible problems, and retain the services of expensive Washington lobbyists. If companies sniff out problems in-house, some of them may be compelled to notify the Justice Department and come clean with the federal regulators in a preemptive move in hopes of obtaining leniency. As one of our informants put it, "we contact them before they contact us, that's the better way of proceeding if you suspect something in violation of federal law, especially trading on inside information and violation of Sarbanes-Oxley." He was referring to the 2002 act, which is intended to hold executives more accountable for actions of their senior management group and financial officers.

Thus, in the more coordinated versions, collective actions are meshed, ideas about wrongdoing doing are shared, behavior executed, information and capital stolen, then hidden away while cover-up activities are prepared. But suspicions can be aroused. An inquiry committee is formed and it evaluates the suspicious and their allegations; if they find sufficient evidence, then a full investigation is carried out, warnings issued, and accusations follow; then internal investigations are launched, perhaps to be followed by more formal legal processes.

Wherever the case ends, it starts with the allegation, the accusation of wrongdoing. The accusation in and around the company can be lying, cheating, or stealing. At Tyco, a ring of top-level executives led by its chief executive, L. Dennis Kozlowski, worked with financial officers to loot the firm. They used corporate funds for huge year-end payouts, art purchases, and real estate acquisitions. At Hollinger International, Conrad M. Black and several executive associates helped themselves to unauthorized bonuses that were not properly disclosed to the board's compensation committee or to the shareholders. An internal company inquiry accused Mr. Black's management of abusing his position of trust in running a publicly traded company and orchestrating "a corporate kleptocracy." Regulators claim that cooking the books to generate hefty pay became common at Bristol-Myers Squibb, Computer Associates, and Fannie Mae. Aggrieved shareholders have since moved to recover gains from stock options and other abused practices by top-level executives. As one executive compensation expert put it, "[T]he only thing worse than having the bad news hit about a financial misstatement or wrongdoing is having news hit the press seven days later that the executive left with $100 million" (Morgenson 2007, 10).

Numeration as a form of rhetoric is easily amenable to fabrication (Poovey 1998) and in the world of executive compensation the words that come to mind are "misdirection" and "misappropriate," along with "egregious" and "outrageous." The outrage over some of the big paychecks of executives is one thing, the dizzying complexities in financial disclosures is another. Business chronicles are replete with accusations about numerical distortions, misleading statements concerning non-tax-qualified deferred compensation packages, incorrect financial information on contracts, misrepresentations of financial facts concerning loans and debt, and then actual routines of misdirected or improperly channeled funds, make-believe compensation committee meetings, multiple sets of books or accounting records, cover-ups, and flowery speech.

On paper, Hollinger International, to select one representative episode, resembles the accusation profiles of long-running wrongdoing and scandals at WorldCom, Adelphia, HealthSouth, Tyco International, Enron, Apple, and Computer Associates. At Computer Associates, the accusation career is as long as it is contentious among the parties in the executive suites charged with overseeing and orchestrating an accounting fraud that ran for more than a decade. Internal investigations, a special litigation committee inside the firm, and outside investigations by federal attorneys revealed what was called a "culture of fear" at Computer Associates, one in which the founder and former chairman "deliberately put inexperienced executives in senior positions so that he would have more control," according to one report (Berenson 2007). There were accounting gimmicks, reporting ruses, securities fraud and obstruction of justice accusations. Shareholder restitutions funds were set up to try to settle the shelves of accuser files. It is claimed by insiders that the chairman of the firm "discouraged executives from meeting with each other and arbitrarily fired managers or employees who disagreed with him." As for cultural recipes into routines, at CA (Computer Associates, renamed CA Technologies) "Fraud pervaded the entire CA organization at every level, and was embedded in CA's culture" (Barenson 2007).

Executive careers unraveled through the discovery of breach of duty, self-dealing, and misappropriation in the savings and loan industry. There were widespread conspiracies involving collective embezzlement, unauthorized bonuses which involved complex networks of favor trading, filing false financial statements along with the trifecta of perjury, lying to investigators, and obstruction of justice (Pizzo et al. 1989; Calavita and Pontell 1990). The schemes described by federal authorities were unusual for their breadth and the seniority of the executives involved. Not only did the accusations involve violations of common-law obligations, such as lying, stealing and cheating of the firm and its stakeholders, but they also involved substantive legal violations of state and federal statutes concerning accurate reporting on the company's financial statements to outside auditors, the required filing of financial documents with the Securities and Exchange Commission, the concerted diversion of funds to insiders and not reporting the diversion of capital, and falsifying in order to conceal the wrongdoing. At Vernon Savings, as at Enron and WorldCom, the company's team of financial experts was successful in convincing Wall Street analysts that the firm was a thriving leader of the industry, when in reality the company was insolvent and on the verge of collapse.

As for agency and who directed what, top-level managers and financial professionals were in a sense "explorers" of uncharted and possibly illegal financial tactics, working alongside other colleagues who were "settlers," working out details of these recipes after they were put into practice. Lawyers for the Securities and Exchange Commission spelled out their accusation of several former Apple officials in connection with false dating of stock options in which documents were created or altered to claim that critical actions were taken by Apple's board of directors when, in reality, no actions were taken at all. The head of Apple's legal staff was directed by Apple's general counsel to create phony board meeting minutes and other misleading documents to make certain that the backdating of stock options was concealed. The chief financial officer of the company was also implicated. He reached a settlement with the regulators over allegations that he failed to make sure that the firm's financial statements and reports were accurately disclosed both to Apple's outside auditors and to the federal regulators. The accusation involved fabrication and cover-up by financial officers, legal staff, and counsel, but did not reach up to the top-level chief executive suite. The chief "dodged a bullet," opined a trial lawyer specializing in white-collar crime cases. He said, "This is another circumstance where the government is going after an easier target. It will generally shy away from situations where the evidence is ambiguous or subject to different interpretations" (Dash 2007, C10).

Stock backdating is the practice of claiming that a company option was issued earlier than it was, when the share price was lower. Stock "spring loading" is the practice of issuing options just before the public release of good news about the firm's performance and future prospects. Both can involve abuse of loyalty and honesty. In stock backdating, a company awards 100,000 options to executives in July when the price of the company stock is $25.00 a share, but backdates them to May when the price was $14.25. This makes for a handsome gain for the executives. The company's financial records are also falsified to hide the malfeasance. Recent practices of asset manipulation also attempt to evade taxes either by concealing taxable assets by exiting the taxing country or by colluding with tax collectors (e.g., offering bribes for lower tax assessments).

Recipes for misconduct are ideas about orchestrating fraud and other kinds of wrongdoing. They are abstract cultural notions about the kinds of crimes or wrongdoings people can do, under what exchange conditions, and the bundle of tasks and responsibilities associated with given positions in enacting them into routines or practices. Ideas about secretly misdirecting funds are one thing; making misleading statements to federal and state regulators about the misdirection is another.

Other schemes involve finance reallocation, asset shifting, and stock option backdating schemes. In asset shifting, the CEO or another top-level executive at a company embezzles money from another company in order to shift it to the assets of a company that he or she owns. This can make a struggling company appear more prosperous than it actually is. This deceives the investment community, leading securities analysts to overvalue the struggling corporation's stock and issue positive buy recommendations for potential investors. Once discovered, the initial corporation, the analysts, and the investment community are victims. At Maxwell Communications, the chief executive officer cooked the books and shifted funds from successful divisions into the floundering publishing and newspaper divisions.

The practice of insider trading involves using confidential and proprietary information about a company's stock to make unlawful trades in the stock market. Managers who are accused of selling while earnings are misstated, for example, potentially commit two forms of misconduct. The first potential crime is earnings manipulation; the second is insider trading. Their selling can lead to increases in investor scrutiny as well as the likelihood of the financial manipulations being revealed.

Take the following example from the data on accusations of improper accounting restatements: A former chief executive at a major communications firm is accused of selling $100 million in company shares for six months. The sales were based on inside information that the company would disappoint analysts' expectations by missing its revenue targets, which resulted in a lower stock price. The government suspected that the executive used internal data to profit from the sale of his stock shares, and publicly promoted the heightened expectations of Wall Street analysts and investors not knowing the true status of the company. Moreover, he designed highly optimistic revenue projections in the public filings the firm made with the Securities and Exchange Commission, further misleading market investors. In this case, from the first revelation of wrongdoing in public accusations until an investigation was resolved, the stock of the company fell by about 35 percent.

A major reason for stock decline is a loss of reputation. On one level the loss of social honor and market reputation is an intangible. On another level the loss can be seen as a "direct hit to the business." Companies accused of this misconduct may internally experience management turnover of chief executive officers and chief financial officers. Externally, customers may be reluctant to do business with an accused firm. Lenders might also be wary of doing business with clients accused of having "inadequate internal controls." Accounting firms working with the company may be tainted, triggering negative market reactions (Eisenberg and Macey 2004). The SEC accusations begin as "informal" allegations of earnings restatements, possible accounting trickery, and insider trading. This can be followed by public disclosures by the SEC that the case has officially turned "formal," the time at which the SEC can begin issuing subpoenas (Agrawal and Cooper 2007).

Wall Street investment professionals may leak information about pending mergers and acquisitions, which are sure to move a firm's stock price. Top-level investment bank executives may tip off hedge fund traders, for example, about potential upgrades or downgrades of stocks sure to affect the price of a stock on the market. Traders may even initiate bribes and kickbacks to get access to potentially lucrative deals in the market of initial public offerings (IPOs). Hedge fund managers looking for a competitive edge may attempt to steal confidential information from firms by compromising directors in the stock research departments of investment banks. Financial columnists may also become part of a network of misapplication of bank information, broadcasting the upgrade or downgrade of a publicly traded stock. Securities research firms may issue negative research reports on a company in exchange for payments from a hedge fund seeking to profit from a decline in its stock price. Downgrades, for example, may contribute to the decline of a company's shares and knowing the downgrade news in advance permits traders to sell the stock short. Employees who sit on the firm's investment review committee – the committee that reviews and approves market analysts' recommendations – possess high-quality and time-sensitive information. They work as the "hub" of information tippers into a clandestine "spoke" of tipees. The result can be a Wall Street trading "ring" reminiscent of the "company" enacted by D. Levine, I. Boesky and others (Levine 1991; Anderson and de la Merced 2007).

The practice of trading around corporate mergers and acquisitions can lead to a wide, and very lucrative, network of wrongdoing. An inside lawyer, investment banker, and executive can sell a firm's proprietary information to others, a clear violation of the bank's policies and procedures. This familiar practice compromises the stock market by giving certain traders and investors an advantage over others, which negatively affects the investment community and causes the corporation to lose money since their stock would be bought at a cheaper price. Wall Street's insider trading scandal involving Dennis Levine's hub-and-spoke operation (Levine 1991) was an exemplary case of favor trading, coordinated action, secrecy, and surreptitious exchange using banking firms' proprietary market information (Frantz 1987; Stewart 1992; Zey 1993).

On the edge of wrongdoing is unlawful risk taking. Unlawful risk taking is not unlike gambling. A bank executive and loan officer places high-risk loans, betting that a proportion of them will be high return; classic high risk, high return calculation. The extra return, which banks demand when lending money to less-than-reliable borrowers, known as bank premiums, evaporates. Into this vacuum steps a serious, if not colorful, set of financial wrongdoings: cash-for-trash, dead horses for dead cows, fast land flips, paper kissing, walking-away money, and ultimately, the zombie thrift (Simon and Hagen 1999, 104–109; Pizza, et al. 1989; Bodganich 2007). The phenomenon suggests that lending standards to borrowers were weakened, that lenders were not as diligent about making loans to potentially fraudulent customers, or, at worst, that executives and loan officers knowingly engaged in illegal favor-trading transactions with borrowers (Black 2000).

In the savings and loan industry, the wealth was concentrated among executives, loan officers, and brokers because the greatest rewards were meted out in the form of commissions, bonuses, and stock awards (Pilzer 1998). Borrowers with cozy relations with the lending firm were permitted to take on so much leverage that falling prices of their assets set off chains of defaults and bankruptcies. The government's financial institutions and the federal agencies behind them, such as the Federal Deposit Insurance Corp. and the Federal Home Loan Bank system, which look after the nation's banks, suffer financial and reputation losses (Calavita, Pontell, and Tillman 1997; Rosoff et al. 2007, 350–60). The so-called "big money" lending repertoires dot the map in Texas, Oklahoma, California, Colorado, and Kansas. The marquee names were Centennial S & L, Lincoln Savings and Loan, Silverado, Federal Home Loan Bank of Topeka, and Vernon Savings.

As shown in Table 2, accusations in and around corporations account for nearly a quarter of all accusations in the years under study (248 of a total of 1,103). Over 50 percent of the accusations on this exchange path involve violations of statutes, rules, and government regulations; over 40 percent involve fraud, trickery, deception, and misrepresentation.

Market-Based Tie Number 2: Accusations Involving Rivals, Industry Peers, and Competitors

The core of the market phenomenon consists of "exchange in combination with competition" (Swedberg 1994, 271). A key to this circuitry is two or more producer as suppliers in competition for opportunities of exchange (Weber [1922] 1978, 635). They are rivals engaged in jockeying for position through market signaling (Porter 1980, 75–87), discovering focal points of implicit exchange, and making cooperative, threatening, and defensive moves toward one another (Porter 1980, 88–107).

Competition for favor and comparative advantage can take the form of structuring the sequence of moves through illegal transactions. Information is critical in both offensive and defensive routines, whether they are legal or illegal. This involves cutting off a rival from resources either from the supplier or the buyer sides of the social field. While the corporation generally wants to come out ahead of its rivals, there are times when the two forces resort to cooperation and collusion among each other to the detriment of suppliers and buyers.

Schemes such as spying, corporate espionage, and subversion involve market peers as rivals. A wide repertoire is found in espionage cases: hiring competitor's employees for revelation of proprietary knowledge, bribery of competitor's employees or suppliers, eavesdropping, theft, blackmail, and planting agents on the rival's payroll (Bergier 1975; Hamilton 1967, 222–23). Corporate rivalry can lead to industrial subterfuge. In a high visibility accusation, Oracle sued its rival SAP in 2007, accusing the German software maker of repeatedly stealing copyrighted software and other confidential information in an attempt to grab corporate customers such as Merck, Bear Stearns, Abbott Laboratories, and many others. "This theft," the suit claims, "appears to be an essential – and illegal – part of SAP competitive strategy against Oracle" (Lohr 2007).

In the summer of 2009, the Justice Department opened an investigation into hiring practices of some of the biggest companies in the technology and biotechnology world, including Microsoft, Intel, Google, Yahoo, Genetec, and Apple. Silicon Valley's companies compete for talented engineers, executives, and marketers; however, there is an unwritten agreement among the firms not to aggressively poach employees from their competitors. The corporations received requests for information, and Justice Department lawyers were presumably focusing on whether companies had agreements about interfirm hiring. When two or more companies agree to not hire from the pool of each other's employees, regulators could raise questions concerning quid pro quo arrangements with antitrust implications. That is, if the accusations of collusion were proven, they would show that these informal understandings restrict the flow of labor in the job market, thereby preventing wages from rising.

"Most companies have a hands-off list," said one director of talent acquisition. It tells recruiters, 'don't recruit from this company. They are our partner.'" "There is a gentlemen's understanding all over the Valley that, it's not that you don't hire, it's the process by which you hire," a partner at the powerful venture capital firm Kleiner Perkins Caufield & Byers said to the reporter Miguel Helft (Helft 2009).

Another recipe is customer-directed bribery. In this scenario, there can potentially be two victims of the wrongdoing. Clearly, the rivals of the corporation are losing out on possible business ventures. In addition, since only certain members (the purchasing agents) within the client company are benefiting from the bribe, the client company may also be harmed. The company receives an inferior product or pays more than they would have if they had gone with their supplier's rival. An example of this was the case of the Other People's Money (OPM) leasing swindle in which OPM would bribe purchasing agents of hospitals and other buyers to lease with their company rather than leasing with their rivals or buying their computers from a computer manufacturer (Gandosey 1982).

Corporate wrongdoing against rivals also occurs when a firm uses below-cost pricing to permanently drive a current occupant or potential entrant out of the marketplace. The practice of market "predation" involves product market prices in which incumbents, as competitive rivals, are killed or disciplined, as a predator is able to inflict large costs on the firm (Salop 1981). A related deceptive practice is to move entrants into the position of using more costly production processes in attempts to drive them out of the market.

Pricing policy practices expose the culture of collusion that permeates business, revealing how a rival is an accomplice in wrongdoing. Here the victim is not a potential industry rival, but downstream buyers. In this classic game, two players or companies are engaging in crime together. They both must trust one another not to expose the scheme or violate the terms of their agreement. This may occur in price-fixing arrangements or leveraged buyouts in which two companies have agreed to collude for their mutual benefit (Stewart 2001; Baker and Faulkner 1993; Herling

1962; Lean et al. 1982; Smith 1961; Sonnefeld and Lawrence 1978). Conspirators meet in secret, learn how to select and promote techniques for bid rigging, make assessments on the probability of getting caught (Bryant and Eckard 1991), and devise strategies for internal bid allocation. One firm's representatives on their illegal committees may "cheat" on the others to increase their chances of winning prized bids from utility buyers (Faulkner et al. 2003).

One of the premium cases in this field is the heavy electrical equipment conspiracy involving steam turbines, in which General Electric, Allis-Chalmers, and Westinghouse corporations colluded to raise the prices and divide up the market for turbines. Executives and managers from the companies shared information and attempted to control one another through regular communication and exchange. Prices were set according to what seemed fair and proper with respect to the regular company success in the market. Since General Electric enjoyed the most success in the regular market, they would understandably receive a favorable proportion of the bids under the conspiracy. Conspirators whose earnings and bid winnings are sharply up in one period may find themselves "talked to" and subject to the informal social control of the other partners.

Norms of equity govern the relationships among the members. The repertoire is one of alignment of mutual interests among rivals. This arrangement among competitors continues for several years until middle managers in the conspiracy accuse one another of cheating on their agreements. Accusations of chiseling and not living up to promises pull the upper-echelon division chiefs into the meetings. They issue warnings about market instability if the firms revert to being competitive rivals. The division chiefs will threaten to pull their company out of the cartel in an attempt to put a stop to the opportunism and underbidding of contracts with public and private sector utility customers.

Executives in secret meetings among themselves are wary of one another because they cannot fully trust one another. They have met before. They know one another. They know how to negotiate on pricing policies, agree on equitable distribution of bids, and carve out positions for prized contracts (Herling 1962; Faulkner et al. 2003; Eichenwald 2002). They learn about one another and as they go from meeting to meeting, they hone their skills. They know who can be relied on (and who cannot). They know there is the potential for danger associated with trusting one's cartel partner, especially trusting them not to keep records of the meetings.

In some cartels, a participant may keep pages of notes from the illegal meetings that document the illegal agreements (Mason 2004), the rotation of bids among the companies (Smith 1961), and confidential communications up the chain of command (Faulkner et al. 2003, 541–45; Mason 2004; Faulkner and Cheney 2011). They learn how to cajole and threaten one another. They learned how to deal with broken promises, how to handle the occasional cheating of their rivals, and what to complain about and what not to cause a fuss over. They learn to balance the legal and official demands of their companies with the illegal and unofficial obligations to the illegal cartel. They are simultaneously company men and conspirators (Adams 1996). Because different "camps," "clans," and "choirs"– these words have been used to describe themselves in their illegal meetings – depend on one another for coordinating illegal agreements and bids, they are often involved in contentious vying for the business of customers. Vying for contracts occurred in several nasty meetings in the electrical industry conspiracy and in the Sotheby's–Christie's auction house scandal conspiracy as the conspirators had to agree on who was to be awarded the preferred "positions" on prized bids.

In a major price-fixing conspiracy running from April 1, 1999 until June 15, 2002, Dell Inc., Compaq Computer Corporation, Hewlett-Packard Company, Apple Computer Inc., International Business Machines Corporation, and Gateway Inc. were targeted buyers of dynamic random access memory (DRAM) producers.

The sellers included Samsung of South Korea, and three rival companies: Infineon Technologies of Germany, Elpida of Japan, and Hynix Semiconductor of South Korea. Samsung is one of the world's largest producers of chips. All four companies agreed to antitrust activity and paid the second largest criminal antitrust fine in American history. There were approximately $7 billion in DRAM sales in the United States in 2004, encompassing a wide array of electronic products such as personal computers, laptops, cellular phones, digital cameras, video game consoles, hard drives, video recorders, and workstations. Consumers paid higher prices for the technology, which was the desired result of the price fixing and market allocation activities. IBM, Dell, and Hewlett-Packard reported that they had to raise prices or ration the amount of memory installation due to the high cost of computer chips.

Four companies and twelve individual executives were assessed over $731 million in fines, with Samsung and its subsidiary agreeing to plead guilty and pay $300 million for international collusion and price fixing. According to the Justice Department, Samsung and its associates carried out the scheme in stages: first, by participating in meetings, communications, and discussions inside and outside the United States with their marketing competitors in regard to prices; second, by secretly cooperating to fix prices at specified amounts to certain targeted firms; third, by issuing price quotations in accordance with the illegal agreements reached; and finally, by swapping information on DRAM sales in order to monitor and enforce compliance inside the conspiracy.

The culture the cartel is controlling is competition among natural rivals. The clash of rivals over prices and bid allocation can force complaints arising in the secret meetings up the chain of command to the top level (division chiefs and their loyal deputies), resulting in the intervention of higher-level executives in the affairs of the conspiracy. Cartels exhibit repertoires of wrongdoing that oscillate between a style of self-regulation familiar to students of professional control in bureaucracies (Freidson and Rhea 1963; Freidson 1975), the "hieratic" style (White 1992, 237–45) familiar to those who study colonial rule (Furnivall 1948; Adams 1996), and tyranny as a means of control in organizations (Stinchcombe 1990, 194-219). And severe recessions can provide dangerous incentives for large and dominating companies to engage in predatory behavior that not only weakens industry competition but harms consumers as well.

The repertoires revealed inside the Sotheby's–Christie's scandal show how price-fixing agreements were reached between the two largest auction houses in the world. We learn how the top level principals at the houses agreed to step back and let their chief executive officers hammer out the tactics of collusion. They successfully eliminated guarantees for suppliers – a minimum sum the seller receives regardless of a sale's outcome. They cut back on advances to potential suppliers (Market-Based Tie Number 3); they stopped advancing credit to dealers and buyers (Market-Based Tie Number 4). They also did away with contributions to charitable organizations as a practice for enticing sellers (Mason 2004). This joins other case studies in price-fixing and market allocation that explore the formation and collapse of repertoires in the electrical equipment and lysine cartels.

"Antitrust policy is set by Washington in two ways: by the interpretation of laws announced by the Justice Department and the Federal Trade Commission through guidelines for the courts and private litigants, and by the enforcement cases that those agencies decide to bring. The government's guidelines are often cited by lawyers and given considerable weight by judges in antitrust cases, including those lawsuits that the government does not participate in" (Labaton 2009). Smaller companies in an array of industries also bring their complaints to the Justice Department about potentially improper business practices by their larger rivals. Some of the biggest antitrust cases were initiated by complaints taken to the Justice Department. As shown in Table 2, these market-based ties account for nearly 20 percent of all the accusations (210 of 1,103), and 75 percent of those accusations are about circumvention of rules and regulations.

Market-Based Tie Number 3: Accusations Involving Suppliers of Resources, Goods, and Services and Commercial Banks

The structural connections and cultural content of business strategies are critical in understanding markets. Through attention to issues of strategy toward buyers and suppliers, the company and its agents may be able to improve their competitive position, reduce uncertainty, and advance their power over others in markets (Porter 1980, 108–22). Here, I take up the issue of suppliers as nodes in networks of illegal exchange (Market-Based Tie Number 3). In following sections I will focus on buyers or purchasers as nodes in networks of wrongdoing with a focal firm and its agents (Market-Based Tie Number 4).

The suppliers of a corporation provide the company with three important resources: land, labor, and capital. Without these resources the company could not conduct business. However, the suppliers also rely on the business of these corporations and can be misled or taken advantage of in many ways. This benefits the company by using the suppliers for reduced prices or plainly stealing from them by way of fraud. The supplier can also become an accomplice to the corporation's wrongdoing by taking bribes, by engaging in kickback schemes, by secretly granting concessions on costly items, by waiving expenses for shipping and insurance charges, by keeping false business records, and by evading federal and state taxes. An initial level of wrongful behavior can expand into agreements to conspire on a multitude of issues.

In the case of Archway & Mother's Cookie Company, mentioned in Chapter 1, the company was on the ropes, caught in a "cash crunch, as weakening sales and higher costs were causing losses to accelerate" (Creswell 2009). The company was thinking about selling off assets and trying to reorganize its debt with the financial help of the finance company owned by the hedge fund Cerberus Capital Management. Cerberus had its own professional auditors looking at the books. Archway's vice president for finance was putting together financial document in preparation for another auditor, Ernst & Young. When this auditor started its work, its accountants were suspicious of the numbers. The auditing firm threatened to raise a red flag and issue a "going concern" opinion. This is a "signal that the auditors were worried about Archway's ability to remain solvent. That not only imperiled the restructuring by the Cerberus affiliate...it also may have caused Wachovia to pull Archway's existing lines [of credit]" (Creswell 2009, 6).

One of the primary resources that a corporation needs is capital in the form of loans from banks. Commercial banks take deposits and make loans. Retail banks loan to their clients after receiving assurances of collateral resources such as inventory. Banks may then become the target of wrongdoing such as the submission of false inventories by companies. This is a form of fraud in which persons pretend to possess an inventory they do not actually have. They take out loans from the bank using this fake collateral without the banks being aware of the misrepresentation.

In these schemes the offender never intends to pay back the loan in full and the bank loses its money. The so-called "Great Salad Oil Swindle" (Miller 1965) involved the Allied Crude Vegetable Oil Refining Company and owner Anthony "Tino" De Angelis, who claimed to have large amounts of vegetable oil. The oil was used as collateral for bank loans. The company fraudulently acquired over $175 million before this scam was exposed.

Another routine involves falsifying contracts to use as collateral in loans. An offender can forge contracts or shop one contract around to multiple banks. This was one repertoire set enacted by the core owners of the leasing company OPM. They repeatedly made false statements about earnings and sales of the company's most important products. They engaged in forgery of collateral documents, lied on loan applications, used a single loan application across multiple banks, and they falsified their taxable income. The OPM tool kit was stocked with tools of exploitation including planned violation of contractual obligations and the artful construction of nonexistent leasing contracts to mislead their customers and clients as well as their suppliers of capital. Throughout the career of the crime repertoire, the techniques demonstrated "the high likelihood" that the owners possessed the intent to violate the law.

In the early stages of wrongdoing by OPM, banks such as First National Bank of St. Paul and customers such as Rockwell International interpreted their behavior as involving "poor business judgment" rather than outright deception and concealment (Shapiro 1980, 18–21; Fenichell 1985, 122–24). In the later stages of its run, it became clear that the company's leasing operations were a deceptive means for swindling banks, and that the principals did not intend to repay their capital debts and obligations (Gandossy 1985; Fenichell 1985).

A corporation's relationship with banks may be manipulated to illegally secure funds. In 2005 the top officers of an automobile parts supplier made an effort to secure a huge loan from bankers at Credit Suisse. The executives informed the bankers of the firm's financial status: its low debt, its favorable liquidity status, and its future accounts receivable with customers. Sanguine expectations were made about the manufacturer's quarterly earnings. In reality, the company was on the verge of bankruptcy. It had already exhausted its credit, having borrowed so much that it could not take on new debt obligations without violating its existing loan agreements. The chief executive and a team of top-level employees then orchestrated a scheme to dupe its lenders so that they could borrow more.

The repertoire involved lying to the bank's loan officers about its growing debt and exaggerating how much money was due in its accounts receivable (Market-Based Tie Number 3 and Recipe A). They did this by (1) creating fraudulent invoices showing millions of dollars receivable, (2) persuading suppliers to report as current income rebates on past transactions, when in reality the rebates were based on the promise of future business, and (3) convincing a board member to loan the firm 3 million dollars. The loan was booked as a rebate, when in fact the firm's team agreed to repay the money. The United States attorney for the southern district of New York singled out the chief executive as the ringleader behind the concerted efforts to mislead suppliers, lenders, investors, and auditors (Market-Based Ties Numbers 3 and 5). "They resorted to lies, tricks and fraud. In the end [the executive] and his co-conspirators were unable to hide the truth" (Peters and Bunkley 2007, 6).

Resorting to lies and tricks can be risky, especially when the accounting firm hired for professional services suspects a repertoire of misrepresentation. In a recent example, an accounting firm in the second tier of the industry is contracted to audit the books of one of the nation's largest mortgage lenders. The auditor resigns. Its auditing team complains that the company failed to produce critical financial information it had promised as a condition of signing the client contract. The resignation is disclosed in a filing with the Securities and Exchange Commission. The filing reveals that the auditor "disagreed with statements that the company made."

In another case of potential accounting fraud and misrepresentation, the failure to reveal information the auditor asked for caused suspicions among the audit team. In the accounting profession, suspicion of client misdeeds and concealment can turn into what is called a "reportable event." In this case, the reportable event was reported to the SEC's staff. In a regulatory filing, the auditors say that the lack of documents might materially affect the "reliability" of the company's financial statements. Journalists following the company and its story of possible misdeeds suggested that the company had problems in the recent past and may have difficulties in finding another auditor in the near future because of the lack of disclosure.

Follow-up articles on accusations depicted the firm as "a troubled company" and one that has been "plagued by a spike in loan defaults" and a loss of confidence among its "financial patrons on Wall Street." Executives in the tall, steel-and-glass headquarters tower soon filed for Chapter 11 protection in Federal Bankruptcy Court. The bankruptcy proceeding, however, is not seen by some business journalists as the last word for executives and board members. Further warning flags may soon appear, they say. The company and its officials are the subject of two federal investigations and numerous class-action lawsuits.

Attempting to mislead professional service providers is one cultural recipe and market-based path. Others include attempting to mislead retail banks and attempting to influence investment banks and brokerage houses. In several accusation cases, the executives engaging in fraud did not manipulate their firm's financial results to meet Wall Street quarterly expectations, although that may have been an unintended consequence of misconduct. Instead, as shown above, they deliberately made false statements about the manufacturer's accounts, the inflated rebate revenue specifically, in order to mislead the bank. This repertoire violates provisions of the SEC's rules relating to preparing false financial statements, knowing that the recorded market transactions failed to comply with accounting rules. It also involves collusion with suppliers and retailers in rebate conspiracies.

Saks Incorporated was accused of defrauding their clothing suppliers in an effort to defraud the investment community. Forceful demands from upper-level management for increased profits pressured lower and middle-level management at Saks to resort to criminal means in meeting quarterly deadlines and profit targets. Between the mid 1990s and 2003, more than a dozen employees defrauded the corporation's vendors by understating the sales of the vendor's goods. The understating allowed Saks to collect millions in vendor allowances. According to Saks's vendor allowance policy, the corporation and their supplier shared the risk if products did not sell.

In this scheme, it was alleged there would be monetary compensation for Saks under non-sell conditions. By understating the sales of vendor's products, Saks was not only pocketing the profits of a successful product but also the compensation for a failed product achieved through fraud. Moreover, the Saks employees deferred markdowns of products from one period to another. Since markdowns are normally a loss of value as they will no longer be sold at retail price, the company delayed, or "rolled over," their markdowns from one quarter to another, thereby inflating the firm's inventory, and, hence its overall assets. The ultimate result of this misrepresentation was to inflate their income by 7 percent in 2001, 32 percent in 2002, 42 percent in 2003, and 3 percent in 2004.

Another recipe for wrongdoing is supplier-oriented credit fraud (Route 3, Table 2). A firm places an order for merchandise from a supplier, promising to send payment upon receipt of the goods; the firm receives the merchandise but the supplier is never compensated. The classic operation is a so-called "bust out scam" (company, suppliers, and buyers) in which inventory is ordered from wholesale providers of various goods (Abadinsky 2003, 269–71; DeFranco 1973, 5–7). Once the goods or underwriting services are secured, the corporation then fences the goods to receivers of stolen property or directly sells the inventory to buyers, converting the inventory to cash. The pattern of fraudulent exchange is repeated with multiple upstream suppliers and continues until the company is gutted and goes into bankruptcy. Suppliers are never compensated.

As shown in Table 2, the third socioeconomic exchange route accounts for less than ten percent of all the cases of allegation (85 of the total 1,103).

Market-Based Tie Number 4: Accusations Involving Buyers of Products, Customers of Resources, Clients of Services, and Investors in Securities and Pension Funds

A hedge-fund manager who has $770 million under management is accused of lying to investors about their returns and the holdings of his various funds, and he is accused of defrauding investors as the stock market fell amid the credit crisis in the 2007 economy. He was sued several times by investors who said they were improperly prevented from making redemptions. One of the largest oil companies in America is accused of making misleading and deceptive claims of degradability on its packages of trash bags. The oil company had a total of 15 accusations in our period of observation. And a giant phone company is accused of overcharging its customers by tens of millions of dollars over a four-year period so that the company could pad its profits illegally. The phone company had a total of 10 accusations. The firms were NIR Group of Roslyn, New York, Mobil Oil Company, and Nynex, respectively.

The sharpest finger pointing takes place around the patterns of lying, cheating, and stealing of stakeholders and stockholders. When we talk about the betrayal of trust in business relations, we know that this is really about the betrayal of stakeholders such as buyers, customers, and clients as well as the stockholders or investors in companies, which one day could become a company's betrayal of us and the faith we place in a firm's promises. This is a thick path of allegation and recrimination.

Accusations of fraud schemes and swindles occur with regularity in markets, as buyers and investors suspend their sense of reason in favor of the financial fad du jour (Chancellor 1999). Swindling investors using the Ponzi repertoire involves a variety of techniques. Style fraud may take the form of misrepresenting the status of the company and its performance, siphoning off funds from later investors to pay and further entice earlier investors, lying by accountants and auditors, falsification of books, self-dealing, and looting of the company's capital (McClintick 1977; Weisman 1999; Slobodzian 1997; Rayner 2002; Shapiro 1980, 21–23.). Home-Stake Oil & Gas, Bennett Funding, New Era Foundation, and the Drake Estate were four independent operations that used the tools of deception dressed up as legitimate and worthy operations. They were involved in, respectively, the exploration of oil and gas, the leasing of commercial real estate, the doing of good works in philanthropic endeavors, and the "discovery of fortunes lost," as in the Sir Francis Drake fortune swindle. The essence of these Ponzi schemes is that the money one investor takes out, if it exceeds the cash that investor puts in, comes from another investor's pocket, not from any legitimate source, such as oil exploration, investments, and schemes with promises of exceptionally high rates of returns with little risk.

The classic repertoire of misrepresentation in market exchange is accomplished through "deliberately created ignorance." Part of the legal definition of fraud (Lusk et al. 1970, 139) is the intentional (as opposed to innocent) misrepresentation of the history of an existing material fact (Edelhertz, 1970, 12). "The misrepresentation must create a mistaken belief in the mind of another corporate actor about the material fact" (Baker and Faulkner 2003, 1176).

In these cases, the potential targets must justifiably rely on this mistaken belief (i.e., a reasonably prudent person could not investigate the truth or falsity of the statement of fact). In addition, the target actors must "act on the untrue representation and do something they would not do otherwise." And the targets of the offender must suffer the loss of something of value, such as money or reputation, or both, and surrender a legal right (Baker and Faulkner 2003).

The provision of medical care is an also a site for malfeasance. Healthcare schemes (Tillman and Indergaard 1999) exploit the illegal seams in one of the largest business arenas and professional markets in the country. Providers appear to have borrowed the recipes and "field of schemes" from major players in treatment facilities, medical corporations, insurance plans, and benefit programs such as Medicaid and Medicare (Rosoff et al. 2007, 469–86; Geis et al. 1985).

For instance, in 2005 the California attorney general prosecuted Tenant Health Care Corporation for a second time on charges that the company and one of its subsidiaries had paid more than $10 million in illegal kickbacks to physicians. These cases suggest that the dissemination of a recipe for wrongdoing is a dynamic feature of fraud in organizational fields such as medicine, natural resources, real estate, religion, and investment.

A California-based limited partnership operation, Fountain Oil and Gas, gambled on its future revenue streams, drifted into wrongdoing, and ended up misrepresenting the nature of its exploration programs and practices, commingling funds received from one well subscription with other subscriptions and misusing investor funds (Baker and Faulkner 2003 and 2004). Instead of drilling for oil, the principals at Fountain Oil and Gas began exploiting their current and potential investors. They drifted into a repertoire of misrepresentation, spending less time on oil and gas exploration and more time on the following combinations of activities: misdirecting or diverting investor capital (violating the financial agreement with investors), making patently false claims (potentially violating trust in advertising laws), misappropriating the sellers' capital for private use (violating the fiduciary trust placed in them by investors), glossing accounting issues that make the partnerships opaque (violating generally accepted accounting practices for limited partnership agreements), and failing to pay professional service providers in the oil services industry.

We find that quality uncertainty gives rise to opportunism. The difficulty of distinguishing good quality from bad is inherent in market exchange. Product fraud concerns the owner or seller of a product deliberately misrepresenting the goods being sold to consumers. Those who are selling a product or those who currently own a product know more about its quality features than those who may buy the product. This is called an imbalance of information, or information asymmetry. The current owner or seller of a product may deliberately misrepresent their product as being of high quality, when it is, in fact, of low quality (Akerlof 1970). We have many cases in which the focal company is accused of claiming their product is more valuable and useful than it actually is.

We find abundant cases in which buyers purchase a product from a company, discover the company never intends to furnish the product and then accuse the company of lying to them and cheating them (market-based tie Number 4). Swindles involving stocks, commercial real estate, and private land development play on victim responsiveness to the rosy and deliberately misleading story line of the sellers. A "pump and dump" operation is a practice employed by "boiler room" operatives. In this practice, telemarketers contact a wide range and number of potential victims or "marks," offering them a seemingly attractive stock, which the telemarketers promise is about to increase rapidly in value. The touted stock in fact has little or no fundamental value on the market.

In the late 1990s Bayou Group was accused of conspiracy and fraud in connection with bilking Bayou investors in a scheme that cheated them of more that $400 million. The founder of the hedge fund, Samuel Israel III, along with Bayou's former chief financial officers and another founder, admitted that beginning in 1996, they misrepresented the profits and losses of the company to potential investors and customers. They also fabricated financial audits and financial statements, and created a brokerage operation that made millions in commissions for themselves while executing money-losing trades for clients. In April of 2008 Israel was sentenced to twenty years in prison. It was one of the longest sentences for a white-collar and corporate crime, rivaling the 24 years former Enron chief executive Jeffrey K. Skilling received. Bernard J. Ebbers, the former WorldCom chief executive officer, received 25 years and Timothy J. Rigas, former finance chief at Adelphia Communications, is serving a 20-year prison term.

With the prices of oil, gas, and other commodities at historic highs in 2007 and 2008, regulators in departments of commerce and their divisions of securities were seeing more oil and gas and mining schemes. Recent oil and gas cases include one in which an investor gave $30,000 for stock in an oil company, but the promoter never sent the money to the oil company. "In February, Hydro-Clean Fuel Systems refunded $87,000 to investors. Sedona Oil & Gas took money from investors without disclosing the disciplinary record of the company. Gold mining cases include a company raising money from investors, saying it would open gold mines in Nevada and California. Investors were promised gold bullion valued at three times their investment. In another case, investors were sold rights to gold to be produced from an Arizona mine, based on promises they would double their money with no risk. A promoter from Brigham City is awaiting trial on charges he told investors their money would be used for a gold mine he claimed he owned. In December, Novus Technologies was accused of claiming it had a gold mine claim worth $37 billion." (State of Utah Department of Commerce 2007). Despite all this money invested, there was no oil or gold.

The executive director of the Utah Department of Commerce concluded, "Securities scams can appear in many forms. It's important for Utah investors to educate themselves on what scams are out there to avoid becoming a target" (State of Utah Department of Commerce 2007). During 2007 the Utah division filed enforcement actions in over sixty cases. According to Wayne Klein, director of the Division of Securities, in these securities fraud cases "727 investors lost over $77 million."

In Utah, the number one investment fraud in 2007 was selling promissory notes "having a real estate theme." In its "Media Alert" the Utah Division of Securities identified the top ten investment scams for 2008; at the top of the list was "real estate notes." Here the sales pitch by the corporation varies, but all have a common theme: investors are told they can earn enormous profits from real estate. They are led to believe their investment is secured by real estate.

"In 2007 promoters took money from Utah residents promising to buy raw land that would be developed into subdivisions, use investors' credit scores to buy homes, develop resort properties in Mexico, and make 'hard-money' high-interest loans to real estate builders. Most of these promotions had the characteristics of a Ponzi scheme," said Klein, "where money from new investors is used to make payments to prior investors."

Another practice involves government regulators as accomplices to the corporation's deviance. This occurs when a government official is bribed by a corporation to get a state actor to purchase their product (e.g., commercial or military aircraft) or services (e.g., oil and gas exploration, extraction, and refining operations). This form of transaction bribery (Reisman 1979) involves inducements labeled "speed" or "pull." The repetitive patterning of exchanges came to be known, in exchanges between aerospace executives and government officials, as a "grease machine" (Boulton 1978; Shaplen 1978). This repertoire of illegal contract allocation was also known as "steering." A bribed government official would allocate bids and contracts to favored firms. The favored firms were the subjects of a shakedown by the officials. The officials, in effect, held the contacts hostage. The targets or victims were aerospace, oil, and financial firms. This practice was revealed in the Watergate-related investigations of military and commercial aircraft built and sold by Lockheed and Northrop. This is the state racket or extortion repertoire.

In the bogus inventory scheme, a customer is a buyer who agrees to accept fake inventory in the supply chain or channel. The earnings projections and accounting reports record these transactions as actual sales, thereby creating the illusion that the company's accounts receivable are healthy and growing. This is a repertoire of collusion with purchasers (Market-Based Tie Number 4) rather than rivals (Market-Based Tie Number 2).

Securities fraud is a recipe to misrepresent the true status and economic value of an investment. It can involve publicly traded companies, tax shelters, limited partnerships, or residential real estate (Paulson 1972; Snow 1978; Bass and Hoeffler 1992; Rosoff et al. 2007, 245–56). A corporation can do this in several ways. The simplest is by falsifying the true status of the company and its financial performance. The target of these misrepresentations is the potential client or customer. The first tactic is deflating the expenses of the company, the second is inflating the company's apparent assets, and the third is manipulating the company's business ventures to appear that they are making money on invested capital. All three of these tactics create the appearance of increased earnings. Equity Funding, HealthSouth, and Enron used all three.

Ameriquest, the nation's largest subprime lender, and nineteen "large institutions" were accused of corporate fraud and deceptive sales practices related to the packaging of home mortgages into complex securities called "collateralized debt obligations." Among the targets were major "subprime lenders" and Wall Street investment banks. Early in 2008 the city of Cleveland, suffering one of the highest foreclosure rates in the nation, accused firms such as Goldman Sachs, Citigroup and Bear Stearns of the following: "Over the course of several years, financial institutions routinely made money available to unqualified borrowers who had no realistic means of keeping up with their loan payments" (Hirsh 2008).

In this case, lenders, securitizers, brokers, and banks were "investigated by the FBI, IRS, state attorneys general and county authorities nationwide for their respective roles in this global confidence game, which authorities are just beginning to piece together... Some buyers say they didn't comprehend what they were signing at the time, but discovered they were left legally and financially accountable – their credit destroyed – as the lenders foreclosed" (Hirsch 2208, 38).

John C. Coffee, a professor at Columbia Law School and a specialist in corporate law, noted that state attorneys general are taking a more aggressive approach to investigating possible mortgage fraud by major Wall Street firms than their federal counterparts. "One area the attorney general should be concerned about," he said, "is securities fraud at the core of our investment banking system. The allegation that deserves attention is that these firms were knowingly packaging these securities with the knowledge that the quality of the collateral had materially deteriorated without disclosing that change." This practice, Coffee noted, reflects "a systemic problem, with the red lights blinking" (Lichtblau 2008).

Through the spring and summer of 2008 the red lights were blinking when the top securities regulator in Massachusetts accused the Swiss banking giant UBS of engaging in fraud by misleading clients when selling them auction-rate securities, pushing increasing risky investment instruments on individual investors in order to reduce UBS's potential losses. In the accusation followed by a complaint, William F. Galvin, secretary of the Commonwealth of Massachusetts, "cited numerous and sometimes urgent e-mail messages indicating that as early as last August [2007] UBS executives knew the market was imperiled. As sellers began to outnumber buyers, the messages show, UBS executives urged the sales force to promote the notes and shares as aggressively and widely as possible" (Morgenson 2008). Glavin said, "The thing that is most amazing to me is what a comprehensive and deliberate strategy this was by UBS. They wanted to reduce their inventory, so they decided to gear up their sales campaign using cash-like arguments deliberately." A New York lawyer who represents a handful of investors said, "There are smoking guns in this report that UBS will have a difficult time circumventing."

In August of 2009 a top securities regulator in William Galvin's department in Massachusetts accused State Street Corporation of misleading pension funds by telling potential clients that the funds were invested in low-risk vehicles, but in truth the funds were invested in volatile, high-risk, mortgage-backed securities. State Street provided clients documents claiming to describe the "Government/Corporate Bond Fund" as securities in the "broad-based, investment-grade fixed-income universe." In reality, as of March 2007, this fund had half of its investments in securities riskier than Treasury bonds and specific corporate issues as stated in the prospectus. In an interview on April 29, 2009, Galvin said his office is looking into State Street "representations that were either flat-out untrue or potentially deceptive... It's one thing when we see a pension fund taking unreasonable risks," he said, "but it's worse when you have a pension fund attempting to do the right thing, and doing business with a reputable company – but losing because of misrepresentation" (Levitz 2009).

In earlier decades, the smoking guns were found on Equity Funding, accused of creating fictitious insurance clients with the intention of misleading potential investors and stock market analysts (Blundell 1977; Seidler, Andrews, and Epstein 1977). HealthSouth also was alleged to have inflated its financials and its customer base. Both firms engaged in "fraud parties" in which the repertoire was put into action through coordinated meetings of conspirators. Enron is another securities fraud involving mark-to-market accounting projections, heavy reliance on what are called special purpose entities (SPEs), inflated financials, and convoluted accounting techniques designed to misrepresent the true nature of the firm's status, thereby misleading accountants, analysts, and investors (Bryce 2002; Fox 2003; McClean and Elkind 2003). Managers at the embattled trading giant would misrepresent their failures as financial successes. These failures included online movie rentals, manufacturing plants in Asia, and natural gas well explorations. Enron's repertoire of accounting games involved mark-to-market accounting and SPEs that made the company look as though it were earning far more money that it was.

In 2008 the Federal Bureau of Investigation opened inquiries into accusations of corporate fraud among financial companies in the mortgage lending scandals. Some of the country's biggest mortgage lenders, such as Countrywide Financial, and minor firms, such as Doral Financial Corporation, based in Puerto Rico, whose former treasurer was indicted, are suspected of packaging mortgages into securities they sold to investors without adequate documentation of the borrower's ability to repay.

Companies and other actors may become engaged in international wrongdoing. British newspapers published bribery allegations against BAE Systems and its connections to Saudi officials involving United Kingdom arms and aerospace contracts. BAE was formed through the 1999 merger of British Aerospace and Marconi Electronic Systems. It has an extensive international sales network. The company was accused of running deep connections into foreign governments, with slush funds to entertain and pay off officials in Saudi Arabia and elsewhere, in violation of the Foreign Corrupt Practice Act. It had won business over the past 15 years with its partners. Recent British–Saudi arms deals took the form of mutual agreements between the governments, an example of how politics and business were intertwined on the international stage. A high-profile investigation looked into foreign bank accounts, specifically into the transactions of those who operated as conduits for payments moving through the network of BAE to high-level Saudi officials (Fidler and England 2007). In April of 2008 the High Court in Britain ruled "officials investigating accusations of corruption in a multi-billion-dollar arms deal with Saudi Arabia acted unlawfully when they dropped the inquiry under pressure from the government… In both tone and substance, the ruling delivered an extraordinary judicial rebuke to the British and Saudi authorities and it renewed pressure on the Serious Fraud Office to reopen the investigation into the relationship between BAE Systems, Britain's biggest weapons maker, and the ruling royal family in Saudi Arabia" (Werdigier and Cowell 2008).

Bribery and corruption practices can result in overpayments, wasting of public money, distorting markets, and damaging the reputations of international businesses. The tactics of wrongdoing are familiar: top government officials and their conduits accept bribes in exchange for selectively allocating government contracts to the manufacturer. In another high-level inquiry, this time in the United States, a top-level official in the Defense Department approved of the government leasing aircraft from Boeing after the company offered one of her relatives jobs in the firm (Wayne 2004a). The Air Force was set to sign multiple leasing contracts with Boeing (Wayne 2004b). In all transaction bribery, the illegal exchanges may be patterned and permanent or singular and episodic. This may involve two role partners in the exchange (an outsider buyer and an insider, or a producer firm buys a customer firm); on the other hand, multiple role players – industry peers as cooperating colleagues – may bribe whole networks.

As shown in Table 2, this market-based set of ties is thick with charges of potentially improper business practices. One-third of the cases in the market center around allegations of fraud, deception, accounting trickery, and violations of government rules and regulations. It accounts for 35 percent (389 of a total of 1,103) allegations of wrongdoing.

Market-Based Tie Number 5: Accusations Involving Investment Banks, Analysts, Advisers, Rating Agencies, and the Registered Investment Community

Unlike commercial banks, which take deposits and make loans, investment banks raise capital for an array of financial services for corporations: they underwrite stock and bond offerings; they manage corporate takeovers, they handle mergers and acquisitions; and they trade, acting both for corporate clients and for themselves. The reputations of Wall Street securities analysts, who track stocks in a particular industry, took some lumps in the years under investigation, after accusations that some were recommending stocks they didn't really like to help their firms keep corporate clients happy. In some cases, stock picks are made by analysts who also are responsible for conducting analyses and valuations of companies in various industrial sectors and for making buy or sell recommendations to their firm's investment management teams.

Rating agencies collect information on corporations and judge the value of corporate stocks and bonds; they put their seals of approval on corporate securities. In 2009 Moody's Investors Service and its rivals, Standard & Poor's and Fitch Rating became prominent in virtually every account of the world's financial crisis. These three rating agencies publicly grade debt issued by corporations and banks looking to raise money. The problem, critics contend, is that the agencies are paid by the corporations whose debt they are rating, earning billions in fees and giving the agencies a financial incentive to place high ratings on corporate securities that do not deserve them. If securities analysts who are evaluating the worth of a company's stock believe false information, they may overvalue the worth of the company, issue rosy buy recommendations to the market, and influence the stock price. In being paid by the companies whose securities they are evaluating, it is as if film industry studios paid movie critics to review the movies produced by and directed by Hollywood talent. The credit-rating industry is viewed as a central "culprit" of the financial crisis, playing a key role in capital markets by rating every product from the plain vanilla corporate bond to "structured" investments. Many securities that had been rated AAA turned out to be hunks of junk – worthless.

There are numerous instances of analysts rating corporate debt as A2, putting it in the investment-grade range, days before the bank files for bankruptcy. Moody's gave the senior debt of the American International Group, an insurance behemoth with numerous accusations in its recent past, one of its highest ratings just days before the government stepped in and took over the company in September of 2009. This was part of what became a $170 billion bailout.

Because ratings are required in so many transactions, the agencies' ratings give rise to conflicts of interest. They issue rosy reports about the state of affairs of the companies they cover, and in return the company can exchange information with the analysts that is not made widely available to the investment community. Favorable reports can lead to lucrative deals and more business with companies. In this exchange the investment bankers build up a strong brokerage client base on the basis of this privileged information and sell shares of overpriced securities of a company to investors. The brokerage and investment houses also issue initial public offerings (the first offerings of shares on the market) that are sold to executives and patrons doing volume business with the firms at a price considerably below the value to which they will rise after being issued.

Allegations of anticompetitive practices were made in 2007, describing several schemes that investors and stock purchasers claimed were anticompetitive, including soliciting promises from prospective purchasers to buy many shares after the initial public offering at higher prices. Prospective purchasers were also coaxed into buying stock in other companies in exchange for being allocated more shares of the new issue.

The result? The accusation alleged that it was designed to inflate the commissions earned by the stock underwriters. These quid pro quo exchanges of favors – bloated reports for client insider information, favorable analyses for lucrative deals, and initial public offerings for increased financial business – resemble a complex exchange of gifts (Stiglitz 2003, 155) familiar to other kinds of exchanges and trading "rings" (Malinowski 1922; Leach 1983).

For many, Enron defined an era. Enron was a cash cow for Wall Street. The energy company generated millions of dollars in underwriting and advisory fees before its downfall. The Securities and Exchange Commission and the Manhattan district attorney's office accused Enron of misrepresenting its true financial condition before its collapse. They also accused Enron's banks, such as Citigroup and JPMorgan Chase (Dash 2007, 2008), with being deceitful about Enron's finances in their role as principal agents for the fallen energy firm. Citigroup seemed to move from accusation to accusation in the late 1990s, and it paid or set aside billions of dollars to resolve several high-profile cases involving WorldCom and Parmalat, including conflicts concerning analysts' research and stock recommendations. It also had a number of run-ins with regulators in Europe.

Clients and patrons are also part of the leaking of information, wherein a brokerage or investment house building its base curries favor and future deals with customers. Advance and secret knowledge about a large trade, such as a sale of a block of stock by a pension fund or large mutual fund, could alert a trader to the way the stock will move. Traders with this insider information can act on the potentially market-moving nonpublic information, simultaneously rewarding themselves and their friends (Stewart 1992). Front running is another concealed strategy for market manipulation: a Wall Street brokerage firm trades ahead of its clients' orders, using information about a clients' buy or sell moves to make bets on the direction of clients' stock. These bets have a high probability of being risk-free. In going long on a stock, the firm buys low, before the supposedly nonpublic news becomes public, and then sells as the stock rises. In going short, or selling a stock short, an investor borrows shares and sells them, hoping to buy them back later at a lower price to return them to the lender, profiting from the difference in price. This could allow banks to tip their valued customers to invaluable market information. To conceal their wrongdoing, those customers execute their trades at other banks, spreading their transactions and thereby laying down a paper trail that is hard to detect. In the quid pro quo of this repertoire, the valued customer pays back the inside source of the tip by directing more finance or borrowing business to the source's bank. In the past years hedge funds have become Wall Street's best customers. They trade, finance, and borrow more, on average, than other clients. As the field becomes more crowded, the premium on inside information increases. We would expect that the dissemination and use of this type of repertoire will increase in financial circles.

Government regulators have investigated cases of the sharing of information about trades involving savings and loans, insurance companies, and investment funds (Zey 1993). Recently, in what is known as the "squawk box case," brokers from firms such as Merrill Lynch, Lehman Brothers, and Citgroup were accused of allowing traders to listen in on the "public outcry system," or squawk box, on the trading floors. This allowed the traders to secretly glean tips about the direction and level of incoming customer orders. The traders would use this information, tipping off favored others to potentially lucrative stock trades. With booming mergers and buyout activity in the market, advance knowledge of deal completions allowed insiders to trade in advance of the public announcement.

Another kind of wrongdoing involving information and leaks is "pretexting," or improperly impersonating an individual to obtain confidential information. Pretexting became part of the national vocabulary after the disclosure by Hewlett-Packard in 2006 that it had hired investigators who obtained the phone records of board members and reporters to discover the source of leaks to the media. Federal prosecutors subpoenaed the records of Allied Capital, a business development firm that provides financing to smaller firms, in an effort to discover how private investigators it hired may have obtained the phone records of one of its leading critics. Automobile manufacturers explored the use of private detectives to damage the reputation of Ralph Nader, one of their leading critics, subsequent to the publication of his book on automobile safety.

In a familiar type of wrongdoing, a corporation uses agents in the investment and finance field to mislead potential buyers of its stock. A corporation exchanges favors with Wall Street investment firms, and securities analysts issue inflated buy recommendations in hopes of encouraging institutional and private investors to buy the stock (Levitt 2002; Hawyard and Boeker 1998; Michaely and Womack 1999).

Perhaps the most notorious example of the conflict of interest and the credibility of underwriters and analysts' recommendations regarding WorldCom, Adelphia, Tyco, and others, is Enron and its quid pro quo exchanges with Merrill Lynch on the banking side, and local offices of accounting firms on the auditing side. Merrill Lynch's analysts would give

Enron's stock favorable ratings in exchange for benefits and bribes; if the analysts refused to comply, Merrill Lynch fired them. This corruption of Merrill Lynch was extremely important to Enron's successful defrauding of Wall Street.

Equally notorious was major Wall Street investment analysts' favoritism leading to misleading stock recommendations. The threats of a large and powerful firm with borrowing and financial needs to take its capital business away from an investment bank unless it receives positive ratings and buy recommendations from the bank's underwriters is extortion. WorldCom became a master at this form of threat, receiving initial public offerings from banks in return for doing deals with the bank.

Institutional investors have accused investment firms, such as Merrill Lynch, Morgan Stanley, and UBS, among others, of misleading them into buying risky securities. They must show that wrongdoing by the seller, not just a decline in the market, caused their losses. This accusation is a claim for classic securities fraud, noted a lawyer at one of the shareholder firms, characterizing the allegation in the following way, "I went to the marketplace to buy a security, I read what you had to say, what you said was false, and when the truth came out, my stock dropped, so I have a claim" (Glater 2008). The accusers must show that misconduct is probable, not just simply possible, and they must include enough factual matter to suggest that a wrongful act occurred. In a recent case, shareholders accused "a chief executive of overstating the business prospects of his telecommunications company." In addition to showing that this executive's representations were misleading, in the case of Tellabs v. Makor Issues & Rights, the shareholder's claim of wrongful intent had to be "more than merely plausible or reasonable – it must be cogent and at least as compelling as any opposing inference of nonfraudulent intent" (Glater 2008, C12).

The decline and fall of firms in the blue chip audit market throw light on the effects of accusations of securities fraud, disciplinary penalties, costly litigation, and damaged reputations. Ernst & Young faced down a challenge from former audit client Equitable Life in the UK courts. KPMG narrowly escaped criminal action by the US Justice Department; the accounting giant admitted to promoting and selling fraudulent tax avoidance schemes. PwC was forced to overhaul its foreign operations after regulators accused the firm of lax controls in its professional work with a client. Finally, Deloitte settled accusations of facilitating the fraud at Parmalat, an Italian food and dairy company, prior to Parmalat's collapse in 2003.

Despite several high-profile accusations and criminal action, this is a thin accusation path and some of the recipes on this route are not statistically significant (see Tables 2 and 3). This market-based set of ties accounts for the smallest percentage of accusations, with less that 5 percent of the total (4.4 percent or 49 of the total of 1,103). There are merely 25 cases of fraud and misrepresentation, only 12 cases of bribery, and 16 cases of circumvention of rules and regulations governing market behavior.

Market-Based Tie Number 6: Accusations Involving Government Officials and Federal, State and Local Regulators

Not only are illicit network paths and repertoires found in private sector businesses, but also they are embedded in the public sector and the political system. Bribery, extortion, tax evasion, and money laundering can characterize the exchange relationships between businesses and political parties, parliaments, local governments, the courts and powerful government actors (Jacoby et al. 1977). The corruption of public officials involves deviation from the "formal duties of a public role for personal gain" (Rosoff et al. 2007, 419–47). Explaining the existence of these assorted forms of wrongdoing usually catalogues the deficiencies or failures of governments and their agents.

A growing body of research has conceptualized the variety of ways markets constitute arenas for socioeconomic wrongdoing in the form of rent extraction as exchange. Rent extraction is a two-way or recursive pathway. In one exchange direction, deviant rent extraction is the extortion of economic actors by state officials; in the other direction it is the bribery of state officials, regulators, and politicians by economic actors. Making markets is closely allied to making states, and making war (Tilly 1985). Economic exchange becomes an integral part of the state as a protection racket, the state as a grease machine, the state as pathway for business wrongdoing, and the state as an object of false disclosure, phony financial statements, and obstruction of justice.

Complex exchange arrangements also emerge in organized crime and politics. The key market and political relationships are between suppliers of protection (the syndicate), the holder of capital (business entrepreneurs), and the state (politicians and state officials). This three-way relationship is known as the "iron triangle." The logic of exchange underlying the triangular relationship between entrepreneurs, organized crime, and corrupt politicians is straightforward. The politician exchanges judicial protection and social legitimating for electoral force with the organized crime syndicate. The syndicate exchanges "protection" of business in return for money and social legitimation from the entrepreneur. The entrepreneur exchanges payoffs and bribes for public contracts and political rents from politicians (della Porta and Vannucci 1999, 217–43; Handelman 1995). The dynamics at work in plural wrongdoing cannot be fully understood on the basis of analyzing single transactions or confining the analysis to single illegal repertoires (Gross 1996). The so-called "iron triangle" represents a complex network of buying and selling protection (Gambetta 1993). It also shows that illegal exchange between one set of market actors is contingent on illegal exchange elsewhere.

The government's royalty fraud case involving domestic oil exploration was triggered by a whistle blower inside the Interior Department. The Kerr-McGee Corporation was accused of cheating the government out of millions of dollars in oil and gas that it pumped from publicly owned coastal waters. Following the accusation in early 2000 federal auditors filed a fraud lawsuit against a dozen oil companies. The suit accuses them of misrepresenting their exploration activities and defrauding the government out of approximately $7 million in oil royalties on federal leases in the Gulf of Mexico (market-based ties on Route 6).

In the overseas rather than the domestic oil business, efforts to secure contracts can lead to questionable payments to supply-side consultants (Route 3) and buy-side customers (Route 4), in violation of the Foreign Corrupt Practices Act of 1977 outlawing bribery and kickbacks between companies and governments. The oil firm may have secretly funneled corporate money to the campaign war chests of politicians in return for silencing investigations. Oil and aerospace companies explored these illegal market (and political) paths, some getting caught up in the Watergate scandal of the 1970s. The practitioners or players in the three market sectors form a triangle – an imagery of social exchange found in Lévi-Strauss's original writings ([1949] 1969) and subsequently elaborated by Burt's (1993 and 1988) work on the bright side of markets.

One of the forms of corporate crime against the government is money laundering for criminals or criminal enterprises. This generally occurs in banks where criminals and criminal organizations such as drug syndicates create seemingly legitimate accounts. The bank then accepts deposits from the criminals and safeguards it within an account, allowing the criminals to effectively launder their money.

In one example, top executives and loan officers at the Bank of Credit and Commerce International were accused of failing to report that certain members of their clientele were engaging in criminal activities, and that firm lawyers and accountants designed tax shelters by means of fake loans and trades to generate artificial losses which were then used to hide ill-gotten gains and then to improperly offset taxable income from laundered sources. In these types of routines, each organizational shelter sought to shield income ranging from several million dollars to hundreds of millions from federal regulators and from federal income taxes.

Comptrollers and funding offices for the Iraq Coalition Provisional Authority conspired with officers of the US Army to rig bids and steer contracts to favored reconstruction companies. A discovered bribery and fraud scheme led a major comptroller to plead guilty to a combination of criminal charges including bribery, money laundering, and conspiracy. General Dynamics planned and implemented the use of blackmail in its dealings with the White House in order to displace a competitive rival and secure contracts to build a military fighter aircraft. This is a repertoire of exchange under conditions of holding the reputation of the US president hostage in return for the contract as ransom (Hersh 1997, 294–325).

In a widely reported scandal, Baker Hughes, a large oil services company, was accused of violating the foreign trading practices laws. The company did so by bribing foreign officials in Kazakhstan and Angola from 1998 to 2004 and making illegal payments in Indonesia, Nigeria, and Russia. The chief executive of the firm said, "The acts, which resulted in these enforcement actions, are contrary to our core values, our policies and our expectations for ethical behavior." He noted the executives involved in the misdirection of payments plan had left the company (Norris 2007).

The accusations covered payments to win lucrative contracts in difficult to crack foreign oil exploration markets. The firm agreed to sign on a compliance officer to "monitor" and watch over the firm's future foreign contacts. The officer would assure the regulators that the firm complied with the rules and regulations governing the relationships with foreign governments. The head of enforcement at the Securities and Exchange Commission noted the following about the firms past behavior with regard to the Foreign Corrupt Practices Act: "Baker Hughes committed widespread and egregious violations of FCPA while subject to a prior commission cease-and-desist order." She continued and said that the lawsuit "demonstrates that companies must adhere to commission order and that recidivists will be punished." A previous cease-and-desist order presumably had little impact on the firm.

Exxon-Mobile was also competing with their rivals, including Baker Hughes, for a contract that would give them the ability to drill for oil on a lucrative piece of land in Kazakhstan. Rather than competing with rivals legitimately, Exxon-Mobile directed payments to top-level politicians and oil ministry officials in Kazakhstan's government. The recipes of wrongdoing in this case are repeated bribery of officials in the government conduit who control access to valued supply-side resources (Hersh 2001). In a recent scandal involving Sao Tome, a former Portuguese colony off the coast of Nigeria, the Justice Department accused a top ranking Democratic congressman from Louisiana of soliciting a bribe from a company seeking his assistance in a political oil dispute. In a separate accusation, federal authorities opened an investigation of bribery involving a Houston-based company with interests in exploration in Sao Tome; the chairman of the oil company was under investigation in Nigeria for possible insider oil dealings involving bribery and extortion. Columbia University economist Jeffrey D. Sachs concluded, "Oil can be a blessing or a bane for a country. The theory was to help Sao Tome avoid the resource curse" (Meier and Mouawad 2007).

As we have seen, transaction bribery is a repertoire of wrongdoing against the government, using members of congress as accomplices to the corporation's deviance. We found that accusations of bribery and kickbacks occur with regularity. We found that bribes are regularly paid to government bureaucrats of all kinds for permits, licenses, contracts, and entitlement. One set of accusations in 2007 involved political donations to a high-level politician by companies in connection with bid rigging to gain road construction contracts, which were under the administration of a government agency and ministry run by the accused. The accused also faced twin scandals involving political donations and questionable political expenses on top of accusations that he had lied in disclosures of political spending, claiming that he had paid rent for an office that was, in fact, free.

Lying to regulators is a recipe of circumvention; bid rigging and market allocation to favored clients is a recipe of misdirection. Misdirection was discovered in the 1980s in the General Services Administration where "large numbers of GSA employees at all levels were receiving bribes and kickbacks in order to obtain contracts, to collect on work never performed and on merchandise ordered but never received" (Shapiro 1980, 9). This is a form of illegal exchange in which a company official bribes a government worker. In return for the bribes, the government official uses his or her power within the government to coerce lawmakers into making laws in favor of the company or to drop issues that are not in the corporation's favor.

In the classic Washington Beltway saga, statements of denial made by public officials after the accusation can be as damaging as any role they may have played in the actual events.

Whether it is in New York (New York State Organized Crime Task Force 1988), Brazil, or Palermo (Gambetta 1993), construction kickback schemes work from a similar playbook of recipes for wrongdoing. The building contractor submits inflated and false invoices and the invoices are paid by municipal agencies supervising the project. Contractors then generate kickbacks to the political allies of the municipal authorities or politicians as the money is moved to bank accounts controlled by the politicians. Bank accounts are then opened in secret offshore accounts. Money is then repatriated to foreign countries (Hartocollis and Rohter 2007). Similar to some construction kickback schemes, savings and loan executives and owners wooed politicians and industry regulators with offers of jobs and careers in return for lax regulation (Calavita et al. 1997).

This recipe for economic and political influence was worked out by the principals at the Lincoln Savings and Loan Bank where CEO Charles Keating was engaged in cajoling, favor trading, bribery, and other deceptive business practices including currying favor and buying the political support of five powerful Washington senators. Federal regulators were closing in on Keating, who was accused of taking federally insured deposits from Lincoln Savings and Loan and leveraging them to make wildly risky real estate ventures. It is alleged that the senators attempted to halt government investigations into the illegal loan practices of top executives within Lincoln Savings and Loan. Senator John McCain, for instance, attended two meetings convened by Keating to pressure regulators to back off. The senators who participated in these meetings became known as the Keating Five.

"Following the meetings with McCain and the other senators, the regulators backed off, stalling their investigation of Lincoln. By the time the S&L collapsed two years later, taxpayers were on the hook for $3.4 billion, which stood as a record for the most expensive bank failure – until the current mortgage crisis. In addition, 20,000 investors who had bought junk bonds from Keating, thinking they were federally insured, had their savings wiped out" (Dickinson 2008, 68).

"Senate historians were unable to find any instance in US history that was comparable, in terms of five US senators meeting with a regulator on behalf of one institution," says William Black, then deputy director of the Federal Savings and Loan Insurance Corporation (Dickinson 2008).

More recently, in 2006 and 2007, the Securities and Exchange Commission issued several warnings regarding the use of derivatives, trading abuses, and derivative debt instruments, the rarefied preserve of private equity and hedge funds in which wealthy investors and advisors use private money to buy shareholder-owned companies then take them private and sell them later. They were alleged to have engaged in price fixing and the SEC was thought to have mishandled the subsequent inquiry. There were complaints of a cover-up after a chief investigator blew the whistle on the cozy, and potentially illegal, quid pro quo arrangements between fund principals and powerful Washington insiders.

Assertions of slush funds and hush money suggest that big firm executives – the pillars of the industry – have failed to reconcile their old ways of doing business with the new code of corporate ethics. Their combined practices involved the all-too-familiar mix of favor trading, false testimony, and obstruction of justice with lax enforcement.

In 2002 Congress passed the Sarbanes-Oxley Act, which required that publicly traded companies follow stricter financial controls. In the wake of this, there had been a reaction or "pushback" by large firms and their professional associates. This pushback is because of the higher costs associated with compliance with the act. Quiet but collective action is afoot in the networks of companies, accountants, and advisors to make it harder for shareholders to prevail in fraud lawsuits against publicly traded companies and their executives. This suggests that powerful players in the securities, investment, and professional service sectors are attempting to roll back what they see as onerous regulation in the post-Enron environment.

In 2004 federal authorities suspected that a Monsanto consultant had developed a quid pro quo business relationship with Indonesian officials and, with the approval of senior company executives, bribed those officials with cash. The money was designed to win looser environmental regulations for Monsanto's cotton crops. The company was also accused of concealing the bribe with fake invoices and accounting trickery (Lichtblau 2008). As an increasing amount of oil and energy business shifts to the Eurasian-African hemisphere, where state-owned oil companies are the locus of business, close working relations can breed repertoires of wrongdoing. Russia, Iran, Indonesia, Libya, Australia, Kuwait, and Dubai are potential sites for bribery and extortion. In 2007 the new chief executive of Total, France's largest corporation and one of the world's big energy companies, was formally placed under investigation on suspicion of paying bribes to win gas exploration and natural gas plant construction projects in Iran. Pundits claim that the big oil business in the Middle East is notoriously corrupt, and the oil industry has a reputation for playing along. In a related case, top officials at a large Norwegian company said they paid more than $15 million in "consulting" fees to members of the family of former Iranian president Ali Rafsanjani in order to win contracts to develop an offshore oil platform. Trends in the bribery and kickback accounts suggest that old-fashioned "grease machines" are on the uptick in regions of the former Soviet Union. As evidence of this, the Justice Department and the Securities and Exchange Commission are now investigating oil field services businesses such as Halliburton over allegations of improper dealings in Iraq, Kuwait, and Nigeria.

Despite the notoriety and publicity surrounding these high-profile accusations, this exchange route accounts for only 11 percent of the total allegations of wrongdoing (122 of 1,103), with fraud and misrepresentation accounting for over half of the cases (64 of 122). Misdirection by bribery and extortion represent one-quarter of the occurrences (33 of 122). See Tables 2 and 3 for the tabulation of occurrences of market-based ties and their keyword recipes of alleged wrongdoing.

5
Finger Pointing and Three Themes: Lying, Cheating, Stealing

In the previous chapters we looked at accusations of potentially improper business practices and their socioeconomic exchange paths or routes. In this section we examine the principal themes in greater detail. The techniques of focusing on market relationships, stripping of neutral and positive content, abbreviating the message, and attributing blame result in three types of storylines or narratives. We then analyze the relationship between these three types and their structural location on their market's socioeconomic paths because "stories are the essential vehicle for elaborating networks" (White 1992, 67). Moreover, stories of breaking rules, and lying, cheating, and stealing, puncture the "veneer of etiquette" governing the social relations of business and contract (see McLean 1998).

The content coding and the subsequent analysis sort each accusation into one of the three cultural types and its appropriate market-based tie. The data collection for written content is guided by a protocol or set of coding instructions for the researchers. As mentioned earlier, the archival sources include LexisNexis, Edgar Archives, Dow Jones Interactive, and daily review of business-related content in the *Wall Street Journal*, *Los Angeles Times*, and *New York Times*. We analyze paragraphs and sentences in order to define what kind of wrongdoing is said to have taken place (Holsti 1968, 626). The idea is to capture and chronicle the key phrases and keywords encapsulated in the public accusation (Ghaziani and Ventressa 2005; Axelrod 1976). To repeat, most accusations, by design, convey one simple idea: they preserve the particulars of their (alleged) wrongdoers while bringing them into conformity with a general type of wrongdoing, whether fraud, deception, bribery, extortion, or violations of law. There are over one thousand accusations with three principal themes.

What follows is an example of lying that illustrates accusation type and pathway location in a market, a recipe of misrepresentation. The chief financial officer of a publicly traded company lies to stockholders and to compensation committee members (Market-Based Tie Number 1, or Route 1), to business rivals or peers (Route 2), to suppliers or vendors such as retail bank loan officers (Route 3), to potential clients or customers (Route 4), to Wall Street investment bank analysts covering the company (Route 5), and/or to government investigators conducting an inquiry about the firm's recent filing with the Securities and Exchange Commission (Route 6). There are other kinds of lying and manipulation of financial statements: lying about financials to the board's compensation committee is coded principal theme "A" or misdirection on corporate Market-Based Tie Number 1 (abbreviated "A1"). Lying about financials to potential lenders of capital is coded as theme "A" on the market-tie to suppliers, or exchange Route Number 3 ("A3"). Manipulating investment analysis by exaggerating and lying about the financial status of the company is coded "A5." Hiding financial facts damaging to the firm and lying in testimony to federal investigators is coded as "A6," and is on a career path to becoming a case of perjury and obstruction of justice, "C6."

There are three principal themes or cultural schema of wrongdoing derived from the analysis of key phrases: (A) misrepresentation, (B) misdirection, and (C) misuse or circumvention of government processes and procedures. These shared understandings affect a market by framing perceptions and actions of alleged wrongdoing in predictable ways. They frame accusations by dividing up the properties of a theme into "slots" and telling us what key words and key phrases are consistent with the theme. The key words or phrases are fitted into the slots or are "fillers of the slots" (Murphy 2004, 47; Hsu, Hannan, and Kocak 2009).

Principal Theme A: Misrepresentation, Fraud, and Deception

The first prototype is misrepresentation. Misrepresentation is masquerade and deception. The recipe is about subterfuge, the surreptitious manipulations and maneuvers that conspire to camouflage wrongdoing in economic exchange. Misrepresentation is a recipe about how to obtain resources through disguise, deceit, and dissimulation. It is a bundle of ideas and understandings about deliberately misleading another in socioeconomic exchange, and to mislead in order to obtain property or resources.

The victimizer is costumed and pretending; the victim is not. The victim is not aware of the true nature of the goods or services being sold. The buyer is in the dark. The buyer is in a closed-awareness context (Glaser and Strauss 1964; Baker and Faulkner 2003). This recipe for misconduct in the market is articulated and dramatized – the use of deception to expropriate resources, property, and capital for another exchange partner. It is also articulated in ideas about breaches of duty to the company, the misuse of official position or role for personal enrichment, and abuse of trust invested in the role of organizational member. It is a recipe for and a recipe about lying and looting.

Misrepresentation is making false or misleading statements or omissions intended to trick the exchange partner. In organizational economics, this type of opportunism is called adverse selection. Opportunism "takes the form of misrepresenting one's background, interests, or capabilities in an attempt to obtain more favorable terms in an exchange" (Barney and Ouchi 1986, 439–40). Thus, some parties in a business transaction present themselves "as something (for example, high-quality, honest, high-ability, low-risk) that they are not. In so doing, they can attempt to secure more favorable terms in the exchange being negotiated" (Barney and Ouchi 1986, 440).

Masquerade and "hype" are critical for misappropriation. The accused has to intend that the deception go to the substance of the bargain or deal between the accused and the intended target or victim. The economic substance of the deal is important. Exaggeration or "puffery," for example, will not support an episode of mail or wire fraud. Most episodes of alleged misdirection are about exaggerations, omissions, concealment, and deception.

In "secret" Homeland Security projects, companies prey on investors' patriotism and falsely claim they need investor funds to underwrite a project for the Homeland Security Department of the US Government. The promoters tell investors the projects are "top secret." The sales pitch involves nondisclosure as part of the masquerade, so the promoters cannot show documents related to a particular project. This type of misrepresentation can be very convincing to investors because it builds on public information about the large amounts of money the government is spending on homeland security to improve the security of the nation.

Some examples along the exchange routes illustrate the recipe for misrepresentation: an employee and the employer in a corporation lying, cheating, and looting, and cheating from the firm (Market-Based Tie Number 1 with Recipe A, hereafter A1); lying to business rivals, stealing business, and cheating them out of business contracts is "A2"; conspiring to steal trade secrets from a company, in this case of an ex-secretary attempting to sell Coca-Cola's confidential documents and samples of products to rival Pepsi is "A1" (*New York Times* May 24, 2007). This can involve accusations about not honoring informal features of economic exchange between competitive peers (Macaulay 1963), thus turning business disputes into accusations of wrongdoing.

This is a step on the road to the criminalization of business disputes. Masquerading in pursuit of capital (faking documentation on bank loan applications, forgery, and phony collateral documents) is "A3"; false statements on applications for commercial or retail bank loans and the "hype" and "puffery" in sales pitches to potential investors and in commercial transactions with possible consumers is "A4"; misleading market analysts and investment banks about the status of the company is "A5"; filing deliberately false business reports with the government agencies is "A6".

Principal Theme B: Misdirection, Bribery, Extortion, and Hostage Taking

Like misrepresentation, misdirection is subterfuge in market exchange, but unlike misrepresentation, it involves acquiescence and collaboration among the parties. The recipe involves obtaining resources through complicity, leverage, and influence; and obtaining power over the other party through bribery, hostage taking, and extortion. As a recipe for market misconduct, bribery redirects or funnels capital resources into and out of illegal networks. In fraud or misdirection, the perpetrator prevents the target of the exchange from seeing through the masquerade. In misdirection the perpetrator openly articulates a clear choice of response and the serious consequences of making the wrong choice. In fraud, the situation is one of closed awareness. In bribery and extortion, the exchange is one of open awareness (Glaser and Strauss 1964). The other party becomes the collaborator rather than the prey, the accomplice rather than the mark, even in the case of extortion.

In several of the accusations described, executives and upper-echelon employees divert or funnel money through illegal networks in order to buy business and direct access to financial and social capital resources. In such a case, a firm hires consultants. The consultants organize shell companies to create the illusion of business-to-business exchange. This creates the illusion of economic relationships and legitimacy. Often in offshore havens with offshore accounts, consultants hide the so-called slush funds for bribing potential customers and personnel with relevant authority on the buyer's side of the market's transaction (B4). The recipe is to buy rather than vie for business, to collude with buyers rather than compete for their contracts with rivals. The scheme seeks advantage over rivals through unfair and illegal means (B2). Slush funds redirect legitimate capital into illegitimate uses: to buy business. The exchange is a payment for preferential consideration from the buyer. This is a recipe of cash for contracts and contacts.

In the kickback arrangement the seller gives back a portion of the contract to the buyer, or "kicks back" an agreed-upon percent of the account. The bill for goods or services is inflated and contributes to the covert and illegal redirection of money between the exchange parties. These are inducements and bonuses for securing valuable contracts the seller wishes to win in bidding with rivals. Secret payments are designed to circumvent corporate internal rules for making marketing relationships, for structuring incentives with customers, for defeating business rivals, and for sealing valuable deals in the market.

If the exchange payment is to a partner, or a payee in a different business, the recipe for wrongdoing is a transaction bribe. Inducements of this kind take place on Route 4. Bribery of customers or buyers is often called "speed" because it speeds up the contracting process. Bribery of elected officials, regulators, and their agents, on the other hand, is called "grease" because it "greases the wheels," or decision-making process, of government. Misdirection is a recipe of inducements or incentives to customers or purchasing decision-makers, so that customers or clients prioritize and favor one firm over its competitors to "facilitate a legitimate transaction that would be completed eventually without the bribe" (Shapiro 1980, 22).

"Grease" is also called a "variance bribe." The briber essentially buys a political "insider." The briber asks a government decision-maker to create new opportunities, reallocate projects, and dole out favors in the form of government-based business (e.g., state infrastructure), favorable regulations, and local building permits. Usually cash is given to have legislation interpreted favorably or to pass favorable legislation. One schema is cash for consideration: to selectively interpret legislation, to buy off difficult regulators, and to ease access to valued resources and opportunities. Another recipe calls for forestalling future problems with state and federal power brokers and climbers. The recipe's ingredients include influence peddling and a precious human commodity – loyalty. The secret wrongdoing is supposed to be kept moving efficiently and secretly. Loyalty has its price and this price is known as "juice." When both sides of the exchange accommodate to one another, the result is corruption.

Speed, grease, and juice are terms for recipes of bribery. The conduits of bribery can reside on any of the six paths (routes) in the market as an organization. For instance, when the conduit partner is a Wall Street analyst and covert exchange agreements are struck, we find executives trading valued and confidential information about the company in exchange for preferred initial public stock offerings issued by the investment house. The transaction bribe recipe runs through secret market exchange relations, as when a corporate agent delivers unreported gratuities to an investment analyst in return for favorable reports that will influence the market price of the firm's stock. This is economic wrongdoing along Route 5: the investment community. Economic and political wrongdoing runs through the regulative-state-corporate pipeline six. Here the variance bribe recipe is about influencing elected representative, government officials, federal lawyers, investigators, state regulators, and judges, in order to forestall future sanctions or fix present economic troubles (Shapiro 1980, 22).

There is also corporate conduct unabashedly meant to exclude rivals. A focal corporation cajoles, for example, customers to agree to not deal with the focal firm's potential competitors. In order to hammer out exclusionary agreements, contracts are written between buyer and seller that say, "You agree not to purchase from anyone besides me." Three famous cases of forcing in the supplier and buyer exchange are Alcoa, Lorain Journal, and United Shoe Machinery Corporation. Alcoa United States v. Aluminum Co. of America, 148 F.2d 416 (2d Cir. 1945) had electrical companies promise not to supply rival aluminum makers. A newspaper, *Lorain Journal*, refused to print advertisements by those who bought from its rival (Lorain Journal Co. v. U.S., 342 U.S. 143 (1951).

And United Shoe used leases that the court believed prevented customers from leasing rival machines (United Shoe Machinery Corp. v. U.S., 258 U.S. 451, 458 (1922).

Misdirection is mundane, easily understood, and is both cheap to execute and more or less efficient in its outcome. More importantly for markets, it is a cultural tool that is widely used and runs through the six network conduits (routes) of economic exchange. It is also one of the easiest to understand and, apparently, to report on. For example, once a business partner (the target) in a transaction makes investments in the other party through repeated transactions, then the other party (the offender) has incentive to exploit those investments by threatening to terminate the relationship with the target. This is a form of extortion that holds the business relationship hostage in return for the ransom, that is, the continued investments by the target. In the field of organizational economics, these forms of opportunism are called holdup (Klein, Crawford, and Alchian 1978; Barney and Ouchi 1986, 440) and predatory economic behavior. In theory, a firm could enter a competitive market and use exclusionary agreements with buyers (Route 4) or suppliers (Route 3) to drive out existing rivals (Route 2).

Recipes of redirection based on bribery are powerful and pervasive tools of covert economic action: in squeezing corporate colleagues to violate fiduciary duties and trust (Market-Based Tie Number 1 with Recipe B, hereafter B1); in funneling bribes to well connected labor officials in return for concessions (B3); in inducing professional service providers to put their imprimatur on dubious documents (B3); in steering consumers to your products (B4); in cajoling investment analysts into exaggerating or tailoring their evaluative rating of a company (B5), or touting the value of the firm's market value (B5); and in greasing the decision-making process of government officials and regulators (B6).

Several recent scandals have raised questions about domestic and foreign companies' involvement in bribery. One securities filing reveals that Halliburton Co. has been accused of using agents or subcontractors to bribe Nigerian government officials in order to win the contract for a natural-gas liquefaction project. As noted above, British authorities opened an investigation of London-based BAE Systems PLC, accusing the firm of making illicit payments through travel consultants in order to secure defense equipment contracts in the Middle East.

Siemens has been embroiled in a bribery scandal involving redirected secret payments to land telecommunications contracts in Hungary,

Poland, and other countries. Accusations of redirection began at Siemens when prosecutors suspected that more than $500 million in bribes had been paid to officials in foreign countries over the preceding seven years at the firm's communications division. At the same time, one of the second-highest-paid executives was accused of funneling corporate money to finance an "independent labor union" that was perceived as friendly to management. The recipient labor union was designed as a "counterweight" to a large and powerful labor union in the country (Sims 2007). Siemens' former CEO and his predecessor, who became chairman in 2005, were asked to pay damages for what the firm called failed oversight. Both executives left the company in 2007 in the wake of more detailed accusations that their firm spent more than $1 billion in bribing government officials in a dozen countries in order to win contracts on jobs ranging from building refineries to supplying power equipment. Shareholders allege that they failed to fulfill their oversight responsibilities to the firm, and the company has been under pressure from investors to seek damages from them on that basis.

Many European countries permitted companies to write bribes off as business expenses that were paid in foreign countries. They did not outlaw paying bribes in foreign countries until the late 1990s, several decades after the United States Congress beefed up its antibribery laws prohibiting the practice by passing the Foreign Corrupt Practices Act in the 1970s. The foundations for these highly publicized scandals are based in "suspicious transactions" and the covert recipes of trading of favors, "blat" (Ledevena 1998), bribery, kickbacks, foreign payoffs, slush funds, and illegal political contributions. These transactions have occurred since the country's founding, through the Watergate investigations of the 1970s, to WorldCom, Enron, HealthSouth, and other emblematic cases of redirection by reciprocal dealing and bribery/kickback.

Extortion is redirection by confrontation and threat, followed by negotiation and capitulation. Costume and pretense are held to a minimum. Masquerade can be accentuated for dramatic effect, but the prey (the "target" in crime lingo) is covertly and closely tutored by the professional rather than manipulated and deceived, as is the case in market misrepresentation. Extortion is a coldly calculative professional exchange in which matters are rarely misrepresented. Both sides of the market exchange know what is at stake and the terms of the ransom payment are spelled out for the accomplice, the target, and the payments induce either a one-shot tribute payment or a continuous pay schedule for overpriced goods and services. The latter payments are known as "premium" payments or rent extraction.

Throughout the chain of events, different actors hold different cards and have different experience levels and understandings of the situation. As the wrongdoing unfolds, the extortionist holds all the cards, has done this behavior before, and knows the drill. For the extortionist, this is work, a typical and routine transaction. For the target it is a crisis, a confusing and merciless transaction requiring obligatory compliance and governed by insanely principled requirements, the major requirement being that fatal consequences can be, and usually are, just around the corner. Absent the consent of the prey, the business may be destroyed, reputations damaged, and personnel may even be killed. The exchange party is told that it is just business. In tense markets, a perverse and pervasive technique centers on the will to use violence in the service of market advantage, competitive leverage, and cash. Naturally, one side of the exchange, the target, is fully aware, or made to become fully aware, of what is happening now and what is likely to happen in the future. The extortionist prearranges the target's present and prospective options, takes the business hostage (in a racketeering recipe), requests compliance, demands terms, and sets the schedule for ransom payments. The target comes to know, or is quickly socialized into knowing, what kind of game is being played and how to play his or her part. Business extortion is redirection of money by "hostage taking." The target negotiates for the safe return and/or restoration of the hostage with the ransom payment being redirected money. The hostage may be a reputation (blackmail), a person (kidnapping), or a business (racketeering).

The recipe of market predation is designed with the intent to increase power over business rivals. The focal organization's intent is to induce the exit of a rival through extortion or predatory pricing. In extortion, the object is to hold hostage something of value to the rival while extracting terms and ransom payoffs. The hostage can be contracts, shipments of goods, reputation, or, in some cases, personnel of the rival. Predation focuses on inducing rivals not to enter the market through use of predatory pricing and threats (Market-Based Tie Number 2, or B2). Extortion recipes also involve other exchange conduits. The focal firm may attempt to extract deviant rent from a customer in the form of ransom payment in return for high-priced goods or services (B4). The ransom payment then brings a cessation of threats and the settling in of both parties to extortion as a recipe for the redirection of capital.

Market redirection by extortion is about steering the exchange partner in the direction the focal player wishes the other to go. It is about exercising "leverage." Leverage is exercised throughout the market's conduit lines, in which the supplier uses intimidation to steer his or her preferred contractors to the buyer (B4). The buyer threatens to discontinue business with a supplier unless terms are met, hostages returned, and ransom payments for goods and services locked down (B3). Future boycotts of business can be veiled threats. The firm threatens to take its banking business elsewhere if the bank's investment analysts do not begin touting the company's stock and tailoring their recommendations to the buy side (B5).

In the political arena, a firm's agents authorize payments to buy influence with local politicians, to buy business access to government contracts (B4), and even to by the silence of potential witnesses in government investigations (B6). The recipe is tricky, for zealous extortionists can shift to exploiting their exchange partners monstrously, and the targets, already serving loyally, can be needlessly alienated, beyond their initial shock and consternation. Other extortionists may step in and steal customers, demanding realignments in present accommodations between predators and prey. This can spark turf wars between predators as rivals over who has the will and resources to maintain the territorial boundaries. Within these boundaries, systematic shakedowns of multiple business enterprises take place.

The idea of holding businesses hostage to potential legislation is political extortion. Elected government legislators make the threat to the business prospects and their agents. Government officials can also hold businesses hostage by delay, obstruction, and potential destruction – the so-called keyword is "shakedown" (Market-Based Tie Number 6, hence B6). Of course, business owners are familiar with these recipes for socioeconomic action. They have their own notions of how things work and how to avoid threats from politicians and government officials. Rather than reactively agreeing to ransom payments to the coffers of the politicians and their lieutenants, they proactively prevent shakedowns from occurring in the first place. They regularly provide gratuity payments and political contributions in hopes of forestalling any future extortion plays from the other side of the exchange. The idea of this recipe is to buy insiders – personnel inside the government – which can include elected senators and congressmen, government officials, and agency regulators. This recipe is the "outright purchase bribe."

Like the misdirection of variance bribe, it is lined up on Route 6 in the market. The recipe is founded upon the idea of an exchange agreement. The understanding is that payments are for realignments, that is, the official will favorably align his interests with the interests of the briber in the future. The briber is banking on loyalty. The payment is for future considerations and services.

The keywords for political–economic redirection are found in governmental rules, and the market actors have to exercise interventionist practices using those recipes, or to use "the use of governmental power by economic actors for their (own) ends" (Etzioni 1985, 173; Swedberg 1987, 113). This recipe and its routines show the increasing role of the state in the economy, revealing the complexity of intervention and redirection in exchange relationships. Redirection is one recipe for wrongdoing in the relationship between corporate actors and the state. This recipe of wrongdoing helps reveal the increasingly important theoretical relationship that exists between markets and politics (Hirschman 1970). Accusations of misdirection are a means of communication between these exchange partners in the marketplace.

Principal Theme C: Circumvention of Rules, Regulations, and Securities Law

The third prototype is circumvention. Circumvention is misuse of government processes. Schemes based on misrepresentations and misdirection – such as fraud and bribery – involve subterfuge and surreptitious manipulations of market exchange. By way of contrast, circumvention involves violations of norms. It is about how to get around obligations as a citizen, how to avoid compliance with local, state, and federal rules, how to impede and impair the lawful functioning of regulatory agencies, and how to misuse programs and policies governing proper economic exchange between the government and publicly traded business enterprises. If there is a transgression of market norms, the accusation making is not restricted to those who are harmed or hurt by the original transgression. With Recipe C, accusations of wrongdoing can be extended to third parties. Third parties are those unaffected by the initial perceived market abuse, but who take an interest in seeing that norms are enforced. Recipe C is about ideas and cognitive conceptions imposed on the entire community and not merely on the interested parties.

Recipe A, or misrepresentation, is about common-law obligations between the interested parties. Recipe C, by contrast, is about imposing these requirements on the entire market community, such as the codification of these into federal and state law. For example, in Recipe A an exaggerated promotion may be used to deceive the exchange partner into buying something of value. In Recipe C the object of value and trade can be stock securities or tax payments. Circumvention of the law affects everyone in the market.

The accusations could include conspiracy to defraud the IRS through tax evasion, making false statements to the IRS, or impeding and impairing the lawful functioning of the IRS. In a recent case, four current and former partners of an accounting firm were accused of tax fraud and conspiracy over their work on questionable tax shelters. The specific accusations of circumvention read as follows: "After being placed under oath, they sought to obstruct and impede the IRS by providing false and misleading testimony concerning the origin, design, marketing, and implementation of [the company's] tax shelters."

The partners also used bogus tax shelters to shield their own income from taxes, and they catered to wealthy clients for whom they devised questionable tax shelters which were shams or frauds "that deprived the government of billions of dollars in tax revenue from the late 1990s through recent years" (Browning 2007). Misappropriation of money from a corporation by an employee is one thing. Misappropriation of confidential information about an upcoming merger and acquisition deal from an employer, and then trading in markets in advance of public announcements of the deal, is circumvention of the rules governing corporate securities. It is a shift from corporate fraud and self-dealing to violation of the rules of the market, the regulatory guidelines, and laws governing economic behavior (Shapiro 1980, 23–24). Recipes of misrepresentation based on fraud and self-dealing can also involve recipes of circumvention. The keywords in the public accusations are about the breach of fiduciary duty, the accusation of wrongdoing surrounding possession of material, nonpublic information about a company's stock issue or security, followed by the accusation of surreptitious market trading in the issue.

Respondents' views regarding the ethics of their corporations were highly detailed in this domain. A financial expert and accountant we spoke to talked about insurance companies' reserve requirements (or the amounts of money they are obliged to hold). He noted how the actual reserves could be manipulated or tailored to smooth out quarterly earnings reports. Initially, small steps of misrepresentation of financial reserves can turn into larger, and more serious, infractions of government rules and guidelines, eventually leading to a career of continuous, ongoing illegal bookkeeping.

He said, "There are plenty of opportunities for what you have called 'circumvention.' There is a tendency, or can be a tendency let me say, for some CEOs and CFOs to move on this slippery slope where the firm finds itself committing more serious violations of accounting rules, you understand that this means according to 'generally accepted accounting practices.' I personally know of situations where you see that the company is involved in reworking the finances, the financial figures dealing with expenses, revenue, capital reserves, and money put away…if you have, say, capital reserve requirements, required by law, and you have a large capital reserve in one quarter you could smooth that out by saving the reserve for another quarter and then if your expenses rise and your revenue drops you can reinstate the reserves to even out the quarter so that the quarter by quarter financial [performance] shows an evenness. You don't want to overshoot on the upside and you don't want to overshoot on the downside of reporting."

At this point in the interview he moved his hand in a steady, horizontal direction left to right, as he said the following: "I'm sure that a *leveling* pleases everyone involved such as the analysts who are watching the financials, the market who is looking at the trajectory of expenses and earnings over time, and other who are watching the company. Once you start down this road, however, it is difficult to turn back. Excessive use of 'smoothing' is at the bottom of this problem. Pretty soon you are managing or *engineering* your capital reserves on a quarter-to-quarter basis and reporting *those* figures in your filing to the government." [Emphasis added]

I reminded my informant that in early 2008 a Hartford, Connecticut, jury convicted four executives from General Re and one from American International Group (AIG) for the fraudulent transactions that allowed AIG to inflate its reserves improperly, a crucial measure of the health of an insurance company.

He noted the following: "The Chief Executive Officer and the Chief Finance Officers routinely work to balance earnings from quarter to quarter. The market rewards consistency in earnings. And while declines from quarter to quarter are punished severely, large increases cause problems as well. The 'bar of expectations' is set higher after a very good quarter. The way earnings are 'smoothed' can vary by industry but always exist in accounts that are difficult to estimate actual expenses. Accounts such as 'allowance for doubtful accounts' or noncollectable receivables and legal reserves for pending suits are available to everyone while other accounts are industry specific. In the insurance industry an account called IBNR (incurred but not reported) is an account set-up to estimate claims that have been actually incurred by policy holders but not yet filed with the company." He explained that the IBNR is an old term from the 1970s.

"If earnings are very good in one quarter the company would build up the IBNR reserve and *park money* until needed for a bad quarter," he said. "The game was to spread the reserve out over a number of years as the reserve accounts tried to insure that there were sufficient dollars available for the reported claims." Often the claims would take years to be filed, creating a perfect opportunity for estimates to vary significantly between outside accountants and internal finance executives. "The only tool available to assess the reserves was actual experience on reserves set up in prior years, as the reserves would run out over time, maybe three to five years. Then the actual claims filed months after the incurred date would be aged against the reserves for the time period when the claim was incurred. Even then the argument was made that past claim experience was not relevant against current experience."

From his experience in auditing insurance companies: "In the final analysis, the assessment of the reserves was decided by the interviews with the company executives. Did they sound sincere? Were their answers and explanation logical? Or were they reaching? Could we as outside accountants trust them? Only time would tell for sure."

He continued with this observation about Enron, HealthSouth, and legislation designed to curb accounting abuses by corporations: "People misuse the financial opportunities or tools at their disposal, and then witch hunts begin for the bad guys, the villains. You find, in the current environment, regulators willing to jump in and try to fix things. When they try to fix things through new rules, tighter controls, you often go overboard."

He then said, "If the authorities, the regulators – the SEC and the Treasury – fail to see what is happening, then there can be ongoing abuses. Sure, the top management is responsible, but I don't hold them personally responsible because you have a whole industry or industries doing this. It is not just bad people doing bad things. If they do pay attention, then the government comes up with new regulations to tighten up the loopholes and you, or the accountants and finance people in charge, figure out how to work around them, which then sets the stage for new or potentially new ethical problems for the business and the industry the business is in. If those in charge of corporate finances see that they can work with this type of practice, and they make the finances look good over some quarters, and no one says anything or objects, or they're praised for doing a good job, and the upper level executives know what is going on, then the company is on this slippery slope, that is what I call it, and in this case it starts with simply reworking the capital reserve requirements and underreporting at one point and then drawing on the reserves that we set aside and [are] not reported and putting them into the next quarter."

Insider trading is a high-profile recipe of self-dealing and fraud. This Recipe C includes the roles of tippee and tipper, for instance, and then accusations or episodes involving "misappropriation of information," misuse of fiduciary duty and securities violations. The latter term, securities fraud, is an omnibus content link and provided the basis for further search of a document's contents for signs of the "role involvement" of the perpetrator as role occupant in the purchase or sale of securities based on material, nonpublic information. This led, in most cases, to the accusation story line explaining how the accused bought securities prior to a planned "corporate transaction," such as a proxy content, merger and acquisition, or tender offer. After the transaction is made public, and the stock price has risen, the accused would sell the securities. In other cases, the story explained the accused's "involvement" in buying and selling stock based upon yet-to-be-released information. This link often tied one role player to another. Of course, in an insider trading case against a principal actor, the accusation will frequently provide additional content about the source and the direction of the misdirection.

After the huge securities fraud meltdown surrounding the 1929 stock market crash, federal guidelines were drafted prohibiting the use of any "contrivances and manipulative devices that would mislead and defraud." The rule adopted by the SEC under this act is Rule 10(b)-5. It states that it is unlawful for any person or agent "directly or indirectly" to "engage in any act, practice, or course of business which operates or would operate as a fraud or deceit upon any person, in connection with the purchase or sale of any security." This includes banks and brokerages. Financial officers at large manufacturing firms have testified in recent high-profile cases that they leaned on and relied on large banks and their lawyers to solve their accounting problems, even to come up with schemes that concealed the facts behind the fictions of the firm's financial statements.

This is corporate fraud and a recipe of misrepresentation, because the company is accused of circumventing the securities law (C1); it also involves acts of investment bankers that aid and abet the wrongdoing at the host firm, actionable under 10(b) of the securities act. In these cases, the banks were accused of concealing the status of the corporation. They were accused of devising schemes to mislead the market buyers (A4) and suppliers (A3). Analysts at the investment firms knew about these schemes and at the same time were praising and touting the company's stock when they knew it was nearly worthless.

Failing to disclose, or concealing material facts from the Securities and Exchange Commission, is a violation of securities laws. The submission of false and inaccurate information to regulatory agencies may take the form of a corporation's chief financial officer or legal counsel falsifying corporate information in a filing with the SEC or in an IRS tax report. These are examples of circumvention by the corporation (C1). The recipe of misdirection is pervasive in the market conduits of buyers and sellers, creditors and debtors, agents and clients, and brokers and customers. Keywords such as securities fraud, conflict of interest, and self-dealing are found in public announcements of accusations of wrongdoing and internal corporate investigations, of federal inquiries being opened up in the worlds of Wall Street in New York, K Street in Washington, and Sand Hill Road in Menlo Park – Silicon Valley's venture-capital row.

Securities fraud is one type of misdirection. Stock buyback is another case of wrongdoing influenced by "agency conflict," that is, conflicts of interest between owners and managers. This is a genteel term for self-dealing (Recipe A) by corporate insiders. Stock buybacks are not necessarily illegal, but they must be disclosed under federal securities law. When they are not disclosed, then a recipe of circumvention is applicable, because these schemes are helping the executives and involved parties to conceal their behavior and the reality of financial dealings in the firm's securities.

In several cases there are multiple accusations of self-dealing coupled with circumvention and similarly, with options backdating, which involves retroactively granting stock options to executives and directors on dates when the firm's stock price is lower. This practice has favorable accounting consequences for the firm and hence, has monetary and tax implications for the company and its executives and officials as well. Options backdating is not illegal behavior but it must be disclosed under federal securities law. Suspicions are raised when the price of a company's stock falls drastically just before the grant backdate, and then rises immediately thereafter.

Accusations of self-dealing may be made from within the company itself, followed by reports of internal investigations; this can be followed by a broadening of the allegations to circumvention, with federal lawyers becoming involved in the case. Regulators may suspect the grant to be a violation of guidelines; academics have studied company backdating profiles and have developed a method for flagging backdated stock options as suspicious (Bizjak and Whitby 2007). We have shown several accusation profiles where the federal securities regulators suspect noncompliance with backdating guidelines, possible violations of what are coded as recipe of circumvention.

In two or three cases, the investigators accuse the top-level executives of manipulation and not disclosing to the investment community and market the price and timing of an options grant. The accusation also further accuses financial officers of falsifying documents and creating fictitious board meetings, in which the options were approved by compensation committee members of the board, an example of Recipe A in action.

We also find many emblematic cases of misuse of government rules and regulations or circumvention. Collusion, price fixing and bid rigging are recipes of wrongdoing in contravention of provisions of the Sherman and Clayton Antitrust acts. The accusation involves covert coordination designed to administer prices and coordinate the rigging of bids and contracts among competitive rivals in the market. The Justice Department will file the complaint announcing that the companies and their agents are in violation of federal conspiracy statutes (C2). When corporations file private antitrust suits challenging their market rivals, they announce their displeasure over the business behavior of a competitor. One company can accuse another of attempting to monopolize, and of unfair trade practices. Federal regulators are not involved, at least not in the initial opening accusations. Soft drink giants Pepsi and Coke get tangled up in private antitrust suits. So do beer makers Miller and Anheuser Bush. In telecommunication, Bell Atlantic accuses American Telephone and Telegraph of pricing and marketing improprieties. Firms attempt to reprimand one another in semiconductors, aerospace, and finance (C2). The best-known and most-theorized case is, of course, Berkey v. Eastman Kodak. Berkey accused Rochester-based Eastman Kodak of disclosing innovative photography-related products far in advance of production. This scheme was designed to affect the production and sales of Berkey's competing products (Porter 1980, 77). Private antitrust suits are powerful tools to communicate with rivals via warnings, reprimands, and reprisals.

Accusations are dramatic events in these markets. They have multiple meanings. In the jargon of social science, they are "multivocal." Recipes of antitrust circumvention can be a step beyond telling the accused they have violated the noncontractual relations in the market (Macaulay 1963). Allegations can be honest indications of indignation. They are public, loud, and clear signals about the accuser's goals and intentions; however, in the business of rivalry for competitive advantage, they can also be strategic bluffs designed to mislead rivals, customers, suppliers, and analysts. Accusations of antitrust can also be politically motivated attempts to tilt the rules in favor of the accuser. They are an indirect means of communication between a company and the government, focusing broadly on maintaining certain basic rules of competition while advancing the interests of the individual firm over its competitors. In sum, recipes of circumvention are standardized tools in a company's cultural toolbox for communicating with competitors when agreements have broken down. They are power tools for communicating with wider audiences about the regulation of economic activity

Bribery of domestic buyers is also a tool at the disposal of corporations and their agents. It is a recipe of misdirection (B4). Bribing of foreign government officials is a different recipe. It involves circumvention because it violates the Foreign Corrupt Practices Act. Extortion violates provisions of the Racketeer Influenced and Corrupt Organizations Act (RICO). The coding protocol for keywords closely follows the application of general federal aiding and abetting rules in which the accusation is about a corporation, or agent of a corporation, and wrongdoing concerns an actor who "aids, abets, counsels, commands, induces, or procures" the commission of a wrongdoing by another. The general guideline requires that the actors had a plan and purpose to cooperate with the principals aiming to succeed in the illegal act. This involves, for example, agreements to manipulate offers in merger and acquisition deals among hedge fund executives in their transactions with clients, in conspiracies to broker prices on both the buying side (C3) and the selling side (C4) of the deal, and in collusive attempts to administer market prices and allocate bids and contracts among the conspirators (C4). There are other recipes for regulatory wrongdoing: making false statements to state and federal authorities, perjury, obstruction of justice, filing of false securities reports and inaccurate tax forms, violations of currency transaction reporting rules, money laundering, and other illegal acts.

Taking money that is under your control but not yours is embezzlement (Recipe A); taking information about a impending deal that could have an impact of the price of a stock and trading on that information, or passing the information on to someone who trades, is circumvention of securities law (Recipe C). The former violates a duty of business trust or confidence; the latter violates a regulation of market behavior. Both involve misappropriation. For these reasons, recipes based on misdirection (such as embezzlement and fraud) can also involve a separate recipe based on regulatory violations (such as insider trading). Illegal schemes based on fraud and self-dealing also involve *separate* regulatory violations. One has to differentiate these accusations. A legitimate corporation that fails to register a security issue with the SEC is different from one that deliberately markets a fraudulent and misleading securities prospectus – a "pump and dump" operation that artificially inflates the price of a stock or other (unregistered) security through exaggerated or false claims. A legitimate consulting firm is different from an offshore consulting firm or lobbying operation serving as a funnel or conduit for payoffs. Exploiting loopholes in regulatory guidelines in order to secure a company's eligibility for government subsidies is not illegal; making misleading statements on the application, such as false financial information that misrepresents the true status of the firm, its past contracts, and its performance is dubious and a recipe of circumvention of federal and state guidelines (C1) rather than fraud as calculative misdirection (A1).

In a civil suit seeking damages, employees were accused a major manufacturer of defrauding workers (A1) by diverting millions of promised bonus pay between 2001 and 2004; the money was diverted back into company coffers. The suit alleged that subsequent to a takeover of another firm, the acquirer's executives surreptitiously canceled the stock options of over forty employees of the acquired firm, breaking promises made during acquisition talks. Executives bribed senior managers with backdated stock options hoping to hush up the incident and keep the dirty secret under wraps (B2). Separately, the acquirer's medical equipment subsidiary pleaded guilty to government accusations of obstruction of justice (C6) after a civil court ruled the company had set up a sham partnership with a minority business partner, submitted faked bids misrepresenting the partner's role in the public bidding, and filed false claims with federal regulatory authorities overseeing the minority incentive program (A6). This stream of events prompted the Justice Department and SEC to mount a criminal investigation. The events were dubbed "a debacle" by the press.

In the American pharmaceutical marketplace, companies file private antitrust suits of unfair marketing tactics; they also, in separate allegations, accuse one another of patent infringement (Market-Based Tie Number 2). They also are accused of bribery in the paying out of hundreds of millions of dollars in so-called rebates to physicians. Doctors buy drugs from the companies, and then get reimbursed for much of the cost by Medicare, revealing several market lines – the company directly bribing buyers (B4), the company indirectly involved in the possible circumvention of Food and Drug Administration guidelines and indirectly linked to overpayments and potential Medicare violations (C6). Pharmaceutical firms can also be accused of misrepresentation of their products and schemes devised to mislead physicians and consumers (A4) as well as the FDA (A6). Overpriced rebates and overcharging of customers (A4), bribery and kickbacks (B4), consumer fraud (A4), and circumvention of federal drug guidelines (C6) occur for the same company.

Hiring a professional auditing firm to do the company's taxes is one thing; hiring it to do actuarial work on the company's pensions and the outsourcing of employee benefits programs is another. Neither contract is likely to result in accusations of conflict of interest, misrepresentation, and misdirection. The potential for accusations of wrongdoing, however, creep in when the same auditing firm does other work for the company such as devising executive compensation packages. There is the potential for abuse in this management and auditor relationship when top-level company executives hold future lucrative contracts hostage in return for generous compensation portfolios as ransom (B3). In another scenario, executives bribe auditors with promises of future benefits, positions in the host firm, and kickbacks in return for favorable recommendations to the company's compensation committee. Paying for outsourcing, tax, and favorable recommendations can lead to opportunism in the exchange relationship in which the company is deprived of resources and subject to self-dealing (A1).

These conflicts of interests and abuse of official positions are reminiscent of those in the late 1990s among corporate executives and their ties to professional accounting and consulting firms; the audit services, which are related to tax issues, overlap with consulting on strategic and management issues. Accusations of lying, exaggerating, and making false and misleading statement on company financial statements became recipes of wrongdoing when the company and its professional service providers became too interdependent, compromising the judgment and independence of the auditor who is in charge of certifying the financial status of the company. Financial misrepresentations (Recipe A) could then be deployed as weapons of deception in the company's attempts to mislead analysts and brokers in the investment community (A5), to inflate financials in applying for loans from commercial banks (A3), to manipulate business rivals and peers (A2), and to circumvent government regulators in violation of IRS and SEC requirements (A6).

When a company does not disclose that its consultants/auditors "wear two hats," investors are kept in the dark about potential conflicts, conflicts that may impair the independence of auditors, consultants, lawyers, and others on the supply side of the market for professional services (Market-Based Tie Number 3). Market ties to professionals are paths for the transmission of resources – both tangible and intangible – and these ties can build trust as well as opportunism. Suspicion and accusation about management consultant abuse surrounded the accounting scandals of the late 1990s. Also drawing suspicion is the practice of options backdating. As we said earlier, there is nothing wrong with retroactively granting options to executives and directors on dates when the company's stock price was lower; however, failing to disclose options backdating to a compensation committee or board committee is clearly a recipe of misrepresentation and violation of official policy (A1); creating documents of fictitious meetings of the board to approve options backdating is also in violation of company policy (A1); submitting those fictions in filings with the authorities is circumvention and can lead to accusation of regulatory rule violation by the SEC (C1).

6
The Ecology of Greed: Hot Spots for Accusations

We know that structural embeddedness and cultural embeddedness are variable and complex. We know they intersect in every legitimate market transaction. Where is the preponderance of the evidence in America's corporate markets of the intersection between these two? Where do markets' accusations converge? In effect, where are the hot spots in the social ecology of America's corporate economy?

The mores of the market specify the "desirable" ends toward which corporations should direct their energies. They are more than generalized guidelines facilitating economic action, and more than agreed-upon arrangements for the convenient conducting of business. Rather, they are rules that "carry conceptions of the good and desirable and must therefore be distinguished from strictly utilitarian norms" (Turner et al. 2002, 357).

The proper quantitative analysis of repertoires assesses both density and direction of cultural content. By density we mean the volume or level of accusations; by direction we mean the market-based exchange route on which they are distributed. The two can be coupled or embedded. They can be tightly coupled or loosely coupled. When a statistically significant number of cultural recipes occur on a specific market-based route, we say this concurrence of recipe and route is a repertoire.

One-fifth of the corporations account for 45 percent or more of the accusations. Some firms are repeatedly accused of wrongdoing, in several cases ten or more times during the decade under study. Many of these are major corporations in finance (160 cases), autos and transportation (75 cases), electronics (65 cases), pharmaceuticals (56 cases), petroleum (53 cases), food (45 cases), and others such as energy, rubber and plastics, and airlines.

Large-capitalization corporations accused of high-profile economic crimes and opportunism are the following: Exxon (22) and Mobil (16), separately before their merger, Boeing (22), Ford (20), Pfizer (18), Cigna (17), MiniScribe (17), Chevron (15), Citicorp/Citigroup (10), Gillette (16), Goodyear Tire and Rubber (16), Anheuser-Bush (14), RJR/Nabisco (14), Advanced Micro Devices (13), ITT Corp. (13), Waste Management (13), American Express (12), Coca-Cola (12), Aetna (10), and Atlantic Richfield (10) (Appendix B has the complete list of corporations surveyed, and the numbers of their accusations). Buyers, suppliers, rivals, and the government repeatedly accuse a small number of American companies of wrongdoing.

The co-occurrence of principal themes and market-based ties are differentially distributed in the market. Tables 2 and 3 display quantitative evidence of the dual embeddedness of accusations in corporate markets. The most intense and statistically robust accusatory repertoires are the following:

- Colluding with rivals in violation of laws governing restraint of trade, swapping information on future market pricing, secret allocation of customers between peers, and allegation of unlawful pricing practices within an industry group (Recipe C on Market-Based Route 2, $n = 157$).
- Stealing proprietary information about the corporation (i.e., its merger and acquisition activities), swapping and then stock market trading in confidential knowledge (C1, $n = 127$). Insider trading occurs in companies such as American Express, A.G. Edwards, Aetna Life and Casualty, Amax Inc. American Brands, American Telephone and Telegraph, Boeing, Carnation Co., Phillip Morris, Reebok International, Revlon, and Resorts International.
- Breaching of official roles and misappropriation by corporate insiders involve a triad of looting from the company, lying about their opportunistic behavior, and violating official responsibilities in and around the firm (A1, $n = 110$). Sophisticated embezzlement schemes involve forged audits, multiple wire transfers into personal bank accounts, cozy deals with board compensation officers, and an array of

self-dealing. Allegations of accounting irregularities and violations of fiduciary roles occur in the sample of large-cap firms, including Marine Midland Banks, Cigna, Tonka Corp., Oak Industries, and Dravo Corp., to mention a few. They are the signature accusations that brought the corporate scandals at Adelphia, Tyco, and Enron under closer scrutiny.

- Circumventing rules and regulations, such as filing false statements with the government, smoothing out quarterly expenses, and concerted action surrounding price fixing, market allocation, swapping information on future pricing policies with business competitors, and deliberately attempting to mislead government regulators (A6, n = 64). Examples of high-profile accusations are Boeing, Halliburton, Wedtech, MiniScribe, and Merck.

- Misrepresentation, or fraud and deception by corporate executives, managers, and sales personnel involves the swindling of investors, clients, customers (A4, n = 61). In financial markets, where prices are often opaque, accusations can be about unscrupulous businesses ripping off customers by their nondisclosure practices and imposing hefty hidden charges and late fees. The mortgage industry's practices surrounding the subprime crisis involved offering gullible home loan borrowers artificially low teaser rates that shoot up after a couple of years. In contracts with complacent local, state, or federal government agencies and organizations as the purchaser of goods or services, private companies were accused of failing to deliver on their promises, providing faulty goods at inflated prices, and overcharging for their services.

Over a sufficiently large number of accusation cases (1,103) the principal themes or recipes, based on Internet archival data of media coverage, offer five valuable views of markets. First, they reveal category prototypes by identifying which recipes most frequently co-occur in the market's six exchange routes. Micro-level accusations occur again and again, as focal firms exchange with their market partners. These are the repertoires likely to come to mind first when producers, customers, analysts, rivals, and regulators think about opportunistic behavior (high density).

Second, while firms everywhere may be accused, they are not all equally so accused, as shown by the accusations that have a low probability of appearing. From 1984 until 1996, 48 companies were accused of only one economic crime. Eighty-five companies (19 percent) experienced one or two accusations and 41 companies (10 percent) were accused of ten or more economic crimes. These are firms with low-density accusation profiles, firms likely to be slow to come to mind when observers, regulators, rivals, pundits, market watchers, and regulators think about bad behavior by big business in America.

Third, the enactment of accusation prototypes of misrepresentation, misdirection, and circumvention on economic exchange routes reinforces not only the cognitive schemas (recipes), but also the structure of exchange (routes). The enactment of repertoires of wrongdoing reveals the division of moral labor in the market. This extends White's (1981 and 2002) work on social comparisons and cultural context of in markets. Repertoires as co-occurrence of cultural and structure offer a return to Durkheim's ([1893] 1947) original formulation of "moral facts" as the confluence of beliefs and practices (Durkheim [1893] 1947 and [1895] 1938; and Turner, Beeghley, and Powers 2002, 342–59).

Fourth, much of the literature on opportunism focuses on transaction governance, mechanisms and structures (Williamson 1975, Williamson and Ouchi 1981), or social networks limit opportunistic behavior (Bourdieu 1980; Coleman 1988). A great deal of theoretical work has been done to model the response to opportunism. There has been a special emphasis on the internal development of hierarchies when market transactions break down. Unfortunately, a great deal of this work is largely theoretical, exactly because large-scale data sets recording the distribution of opportunism and accusations of market wrongdoing are rare and difficult to obtain. The distribution of opportunistic behavior in social systems in general and markets in particular is unknown.

The data presented here on over 400 firms and over a thousand allegations are of special utility because they permit us to get much closer to the phenomena of interest. The focus on firm-specific accusations of lying, cheating, and stealing more accurately reflect *local* market interface situations (White 1992), the ones firms actually experience. Given the rarity of empirical analysis of accusations of economic crime and the necessity of including the paths along with it flows – in order to understand recipes and routes together – this is an important empirical contribution to the understanding of mechanisms behind actions against the market.

A most-utilized route for taking umbrage and making accusations of misconduct is market transactions between buyers and sellers. The purchaser nexus is followed by accusations in and around the company itself (insider trading, looting, embezzlement, self-dealing) with 22 percent of the occurrences. The third accusation route surrounds industry peers, and other corporations as rivals or competitors (19 percent). The majority of these cases are generated by the government in the form of accusations found in keywords such as restraint of trade, collusion, price fixing, and market allocation.

The three market-based routes account for three-quarters of all the accusations in over a decade of business transactions involving more than 400 high-capitalization companies in the American economy. By contrast, there are five or six thinner recipes and routes accounting for a small number of occurrences. While firms everywhere may be accused of business dishonesty and transgressions of norms of economic behavior, they are not all equally subject to these allegations.

The moral context of the market reveals a strong affinity between the ideas about accusations (the recipes or principal themes) and the propensity of group members to be the recipients of those ideas in specific exchange transactions (the routes or market-based ties). This analysis provides an empirical base for the growing theoretical work on the enactment of market as "context" (White 2002), revealed in the double-embeddedness of cultural repertoires (recipes) and structural routes (market-based ties).

Fifth, and finally, accusations of fraud, bribery, and corruption pose substantial risks for the managements of corporations, as top executives recognize the risk allegations of misconduct bring to their brands and reputations. In Europe, for example, attitudes towards bribery and payoffs appear to be hardening in the wake of scandals at Alstom, the French engineering giant, accused of paying hundreds of millions of dollars in bribes to gain contracts in South America from 1995 to 2003, and at BAE Systems, the British defense, security, and aerospace company, accused of payments involving arms sales to Saudi Arabia. Richard Cellini, a top executive at Integrity Interactive, a consulting firm in Massachusetts, said, "What you are seeing now is an increased sensibility among global companies that the reputational damage of bribery allegations has become much more significant than any actual legal consequences." He also noted that his firm, which advises clients such as BP, Coca-Cola, Novartis, and Adidas, is operating in a new atmosphere with respect to allegations of corporate wrongdoing. He suggests that with the increased speed of communication, accusations can have profound and lasting affects on firms. Before the investigation is announced, even before the formal indictments are handed down, and before the convictions of economic crime, allegations are aired. The airing is accentuated in the print media and the business news along with Internet and the 24-hour cable news cycle. "The rules of the game have changed," Cellini speculates. "In the age of the Internet, the brand damage from these allegations is sustained overnight even if the actual legal facts are established months or even years later" (Clark 2008).

Technology and economic factors are clearly critical in understanding the nature of accusations of opportunistic action in economic enterprises, but the form or structure of opportunism can also be detected through actual patterns of market interaction in society. This suggests further that the economic theory of opportunism may in fact be a theory based on, and only well suited to, neither the analysis of responses to opportunistic behavior, not the structural location of it nor the differential distribution of it in actual markets.

It seems that Williamson's analysis of opportunism concentrates on governance structures as responses to opportunistic behavior; in his treatment, opportunistic behavior occurs as uncertainty within the marketplace increases. The more uncertainty, the greater the likelihood that exchange partners will cheat. The more cheating, the less reliable and less efficient the market becomes. The less efficient the exchanges, the more businesses reorganize to deal with the inefficiencies. They reorganize through creating a "governance structure" that internalizes the market interface transactions, bringing those transactions inside the firm.

Institutional theory calls attention to the importance of the external institutional environment for shaping organizational structures. According to institutional theory, corporations are embedded in larger legal and normative environments, and the characteristics of these environments influence organizational structures and behavior (DiMaggio and Powell 1983; Meyer and Rowan 1977). Most theoretical support for this perspective comes from studies documenting organizations' responses to opportunism. This is a reception theory of opportunism, stressing how corporations respond to cheating. In this view, opportunism creates a demand for changes in organizational structure. Our emphasis has been on the supply of opportunism in a market as an organizational field, and we stress the differential distribution of lying, cheating, and stealing across multiple market interfaces – the focal firm in interaction with its suppliers, buyers, peers, analysts, and state and local regulators. We offer a paradigm shift, a shift in theoretical emphasis from variations on the "demand" or reception side of lying and cheating (organizational governance in response to opportunism) to an emphasis on production-side or supply-side dynamics (the recipes constituting opportunism and its distribution in markets).

A fundamental insight of a supply-side theory of opportunism (as opposed to the reception or response-side theory) is that accusations of cheating and stealing are cultural (recipes) and structural (routes) activities in themselves, and can be studied apart from the responses of organizations. Accusations become repertoires when robust patterns of recipes occur on specific market routes.

We expect institutional environments to produce variation in accusations by also affecting buyers' and sellers' awareness of their rights and regulatory agents' assessment of the legal implications of allegations of wrongdoing. Organizations embedded in market exchanges that foster norms of reciprocity, openness, and fairness should increase buyers' and sellers' consciousness by reminding them of their rights and thus making them more likely to air their complaints, grievances, and allegations (such as fraud).

A supply-side theory proposes that for there to be a high level of opportunism in a market, many efficient and eager firms must compete in the market through illegal behavior – lying, cheating, and stealing – as well as legal behavior. State regulation is a primary factor determining the extent of competition in markets. To the degree that the state regulates corporate behavior, thus restricting competition in the supply side of legal action, illegal action will also be affected, and overall levels of lying and cheating will be low. However, when the state loosens the reins and permits a freer market for legal behavior, misrepresentation, misdirection, and circumvention will also emerge and overall levels of opportunism will be high. Seen from this perspective, high levels of opportunism are not anomalous, but are the expected results of the high levels of competition that exist in the relatively unregulated American economy.

As an immense body of research has demonstrated, white-collar and corporate economic crime (however measured) are, if anything, more vigorous than ever and seem entirely immune to the efforts of local, state, and federal regulations, rules, and regulators. But the state of research in this area is still best described as inchoate. Despite widespread acceptance of the idea that "economic" and "noneconomic" factors play a role in markets, only a handful of studies have made genuine progress toward understanding the significance of these factors in crimes by and against corporations.

A reason for this state of affairs is that – often because of data considerations – researchers have typically used criminal disposition or "official crimes" to measure corporate wrongdoing. The initial complaint or charge, or, even more fundamentally, the initial accusations of transgression, are glossed over in favor of final, formal rulings. This in turn means that two key issues – accusation content and economic pathway – have received insufficient attention in theory and research.

Consistent with the expectations of the new paradigm, we find statistically robust results showing accusations of corporate crime as the first and highly public signs of economic wrongdoing. These socioeconomic accusations are densely populated in specific economic transactions where the corporation is used as an economic weapon. Accusations occur inside the firm when the corporation is a victim of alleged wrongdoing. The connection between organizational routes of the opportunistic efforts and the culture of recipes of wrongdoing permits an examination of the extent to which structure and culture interact in affecting the moral context of the market.

7
The Repertoires of Wrongdoing

Life being all inclusion and confusion, and art being all discrimination and selection, the latter, in search of the hard latent value with which alone it is concerned, sniffs round the mass as instinctively and unerringly as a dog suspicious of some buried bone.

– Henry James

The study of accusations is a process of sniffing and finding. There is "hard latent value" to be found in the art of the intermediate, between weak informal complaints and strong criminal charges and sanctions. Allegations in this intermediary or "goldilocks" position help reveal the moral order of the market in which violations of the code of business conduct evoke reactions that tend to publicly announce, and thereby reinforce, the norms.

Accusations pervade our news headlines and public affairs, but how should we evaluate these when they occur in economic transactions? All established markets operate with institutional rules governing the roles and responsibilities of market actors and the rules of exchange. Here we see that something has gone afoul in business and uncover the rules and understandings governing economic exchange by finding where and how people take umbrage and complain about the behavior of their exchange partners. Taking umbrage directs us to situations in which people complain that things are not as they should be, thereby revealing the rules of exchange, their interests, and their ideas about misrepresentation and misdirection.

As noted in Chapter 1, the market is a social institution. The institutionalization of a market is a "political–cultural construction" reflecting power struggles among firms attempting to control the market and ensure their survival (Fligstein 1996). The state plays a role in the building, maintenance, and culture of markets, reflecting the importance of circumvention of rules and regulations.

The power struggle among firms includes both a "struggle of competition" among rivals "vying for opportunities of exchange" (Weber [1922] 1978, 635) and an "interest struggle" between buyer and seller engaged in an actual exchange relationship (Swedberg 1994, 264–65; Baker, Faulkner, Fisher 1998, 170–72). We show that the dynamics of vying for opportunities of exchange can turn into lying to customers, suppliers, Wall Street analysts, and agents of the state.

Previous work on the sociology of markets has paid scant attention to the idea that important aspects of exchange might be related to opportunism and illegal behavior. All three cognitive schemas or recipes – misrepresentation, misdirection, and circumvention – influence exchange in market ties, but their importance varies. The accusations of violations of rules or shared understandings reveal the power struggle between buyers and sellers and the role of the state. In the power struggle between buyers and sellers, each side mobilizes resources to enact its particular interests in the (in)stability of exchange culture and relationships. Generally, sellers are accused of lying and cheating more than buyers; and sellers are also accused of restraint of trade and collusion in order to shield them from what is called "the discipline of competition." Accusations of wrongdoing enhance a sociological understanding of a defining principle of modern society – the right to make and break relationships (Coleman 1974, 24–25). The prelude to breaking of market relationships is often found in the accusation of economic wrongdoing and allegation of crime against a corporation.

Repertoire is back on the sociological agenda. The so-called culture turn in social science and socioeconomics (Friedland and Mohr 2004; Faulkner 2002; Sewell 1999) has invigorated a long-standing interest in cultural recipes and routines (Goodenough 1981). It has also renewed analytic interest in agency and modeling the social actor's choices and selections for turning ideas and understandings into practices in specific situations. People doing empirical social science now take the concept of repertoire as a given (Meyer and Rowan 1977 and 1978). Politics displays repertoires of contention in collective actions (Tilly 1995a and 1995b).

Lovers make use of romantic language and action (Swidler 2003). Jazz musicians use shared repertoires of songs to organize their performances (Faulkner and Becker 2004).

In the socioeconomic literature, managers rely on repertoires of trust to run enterprises (Mizrachi, Drori, and Anspach 2007). Participants in markets use the three major control repertoires of price, trust, and authority to govern transactions (Bradach and Eccles 1989). Corporate players in markets can also use repertoires of wrongdoing to opportunistically take advantage of prices and trust in economic exchanges as well as abuse positions of authority in order to exercise their will over others in business dealings. This is a cultural context of market repertoires.

The illustrations of selecting and applying a recipe of wrongdoing in a given social context emphasize "a general way of organizing action… that might allow one to reach several *different* life goals" (Swidler 1986, 277, emphasis added). A market actor's goal of "self-interest seeking with guile" is his manipulation of trust and social skills (Williamson 1975, 26), which is necessary for market exchange. Repertoires of wrongdoing are (1) sets of illegal economic exchanges, (2) enacted by role occupants, (3) within production markets of publicly traded corporations, in which (4) the production market is constituted by the corporation, rivals, suppliers, buyers, financial banks, securities analysts, state investigators, and regulators.

There are three distinct types of repertoires: self-dealing and fraud, bribery and extortion, and regulative wrongdoing. These three may be intertwined, overlapping, and intermixed. In the six market-based ties there are hybrids and combinations of the three. Price dominates, by means of repertoires of fraud, bribery, and self-dealing, the horizontal production interfaces between suppliers and buyers. It also dominates so-called gift exchanges of information, preferred status reports, initial public offerings, and other special considerations in the informal – and at times illegal – trading behavior between exchange partners.

Authority and control, on the other hand, dominate the vertical interface between state and corporation by means of other repertoires, that is, threat, hostage taking, and ransom paying are intertwined in the negotiation, buying and selling of state-related goods and services. In both conduit planes, economic exchange is carried through a mixture of illegal repertoires as well as legal repertoires of obligation, trust, and price.

Wrongdoing rarely affects only one target, and it is not necessarily only one illegal routine. Illegal repertoires as defined above undermine, attack, and perhaps destroy legitimate entrepreneurship in markets. Because it involves market actors observing and responding to one another in the putting together of novel combinations of resources, accusatory repertoires are closely followed market events just because they represent a potentially destructive side of entrepreneurship (Baumol 1993). That is, they attract attention, some of it – most of it – unwanted. Accusatory repertoires go against the grain of the market as a social structure.

Institutional theorists have argued for the advantages of conformity. In this sense, large-cap corporations benefit by following typical legal repertoires and from having no allegations against them, for this profile is likely to be seen as attractive and legitimate by customers, competitors, suppliers, and regulators. From this perspective, the defiance of convention or transgression of the norms of market exchange often carry with them the hazards of novelty and unpredictability, with the possibility of attracting the attention of state and national regulators, antagonizing current customers, scaring off potential clients, stirring up industry rivals, and possibly alienating powerful corporate stakeholders. As Wellman and Berkowitz (1988, 222) state, "markets are social structures and not the spontaneous products of aggregated dyadic exchanges…The ways in which actors observe and respond to others – the essence of a market – can be determined in the same fashion as any other socially structured activity."

We have shown that a corporation's activities of alleged wrongdoing vary by social structural location (market-based ties of exchange) and cultural content (theme). Practices rise and fall, come into and out of favor in markets. Each decade has a favored type of illegal corporate crime. The most social and statistically significant accusatory repertoires are the following: corporate deception, misrepresentation, accounting trickery, embezzlement, and looting in and around the business itself (market-based ties on Route 1 and Recipe A); collusion, price-fixing and circumvention of antitrust (market-based ties on Route 2 and Recipe C); and bribery of government officials and regulators (market-based ties on Route 6 and Recipe B).

By far the most active voices are customers, purchasers, and clients. The most explicit and morally charged attributions of blame are on Market-Based Exchange Route 4 with the three recipes: A, B, and C. Fully, a third of all accusations of wrongdoing involve a company selling products and services for customers, followed by allegations of crime by and against the corporation. In the organizational market we studied, the producer-to-seller nexus is the hot zone in which repertoires of contention occur.

Following Tilly, by repertoire of contention we mean "a limited set of routines that are learned, *shared* and acted out through a relatively deliberate process of choice (Tilly 1995b, 42, emphasis added). We find this zone of contention one in which a predominance of "pairs of actors make and receive claims bearing on each other's interest" (Tilly 1995b, 43). This market-based tie is a hotly contested part of the American market in which members of a group making claims and attempting to resolve problems they may be facing without invoking the law, formally enact accusations of wrongdoing. Thus, the idea of repertoires of contention is of importance to the social analysis of economics as well as politics.

These findings may be controversial. Some scholars of corporate and organizational crime will be skeptical of focusing on accusations rather than crime. These are, they would argue, "*mere* accusations," not the real thing – corporate crime, that is, the eventual disposition of the criminal case. They will also be skeptical of quantifying accusations, rather than quantifying crime. They may feel that the application of numbers to the early stages of allegation abstracts and distorts the "real" content of white-collar crime. Despite such critics, a convincing case can be made for our quantifying the accusations of corporate wrongdoing. The cases and statistics allied with the qualitative data, despite their apparent superficiality, result in new insights. Moreover, the data not only provide an initial window into the mechanisms governing warnings, but in doing so they keep us very close to the marketplace processes through which exchange is enacted, promises made, and violations of norms conducted. In this sense, they overcome some of the limitations inherent in research that focuses exclusively on the end product of illegal action, national quantitative data on crime rates, and industry level cases of white-collar crime as opposed to local and market processes.

In addition, qualitative archival data have been used to illustrate the quantitative results. Our aim has been to explore the empirical foundations of repertoire itself, showing the breadth and depth of cultural recipes and their market-based routes. By drawing on a thousand accusation events over twenty years in the American economy, we see where coupling of culture and structure occur at specific market interfaces.

As we have noted throughout, corporate crimes and their context reveal the so-called dark side of market alliances (Hirsch 2003; Hirsch and Pozner 2006), such as conflicts of interest among professional firms and their clients (Levitt and Dwyer 2002; Hayward and Boeker 1998), credibility of underwriter analyst recommendations (Michaely and

Womack 1999), fraud in oil and gas speculation (Baker and Faulkner 2004), and securities violations (Shapiro 1984). Repertoires reveal the dark side of organizations and their misconduct (Vaughan 1999, 287–92). Practices have repercussions not only for other practitioners as accomplices and targets, but also for the field itself, as in the diffusion of illegal practices, the emergence of keywords of wrongdoing (i.e., "pretexting," "front-running," "smoothing," "paper walking," "channel stuffing," and others), the responses of regulatory agencies, and the ebb and flow of scandal and reform (Reisman 1979).

Principal themes or organizational recipes are cognitive schemas about how to do things. Routines are the enactment of recipes into practice. With these cultural recipes, market actors cope with and make sense of market opportunities and pressures that constrain their actions. Different social locations in the market provide them with different cultural tools to deal with these situations. Recipes are enacted in the sense that they are "deployed," "mobilized," or "used" – the words are interchangeable in so-called "toolkit theory" (Swidler 2001). The techniques of shaping the public accusation – *focusing, stripping, abbreviating, attributing* – are fresh and sharp tools, rather than the bent nails, blunt saws, and dried glue found at the bottom of the toolkits used for the study of corporate and white-collar crime.

There are three principal themes or recipes for allegations about the turning of legitimate exchange into wrongful exchange: *misrepresentation* (self-dealing, fraud, embezzlement, looting, and insider trading), *misdirection* (bribery, kickbacks, secret inducements, hostage taking, and extortion), and *circumvention* (violations of common-law obligations codified in federal and state substantive law, regulatory norms, and rules). Circumvention also includes accusations and charges of perjury and obstruction of justice. Misrepresentation, misdirection, and circumvention are enacted under the guise of market exchange. The three recipes present abstract cultural notions about the categories of business misconduct and market wrongdoing, the bundle of tasks and responsibilities that are involved, and the strategies for expropriation at the point of market exchange. Recipes are enacted into routines or practices on organizational pathways revealing repertoires of wrongdoing in markets.

Hundreds of enactments show the distribution of repertoires and the odds that a particular recipe will appear with its corresponding routine. The distribution of recipes and routines reveal the oft cited but underexamined dynamic of structure from culture. Allegation is communication. It is communication about cognitive templates and normative rules of the game in commercial market exchange. Accusation through keywords is an instrument in the cultural toolkit of capitalism's players. The accusation as instrument is flexible, creative, and improvisatory. Accusations stand between loosely coupled, informal, invisible handshake agreements and tightly coupled, formal, public, contractual, and legal agreements.

Circumstances can turn otherwise legitimate repertoires into illegitimate ones: for instance, competitors might openly compare notes on all kinds of industry trends and then start to secretly collaborate on pricing policies and bid assignments. As shown above, a repertoire may be improvisational, incremental, and cumulative.

If improvisational, the social actors develop new combinations of routines as they improvise their way into illegality, rather than conforming to a predetermined criminal strategy or plan.

If cumulative, the securing and expanding of exchange and exchange partners reveals to them the elastic line dividing legitimate from illegitimate.

If incremental, a series of steps that are individually legitimate lead to a career of wrongdoing; some financial repertoires against lenders of capital can start off as technical inconsistencies and small indiscretions that then turn into multiple frauds, such as false financial statements, conspiracy, signature forgery, bribery and kickback, money laundering, tax evasion, and obstruction of justice. When firms begin to work together and take part in joint ventures, executives form personal bonds and rivalry dissipates. Fierce competition yields to discussions about industry conditions and prices. Market talk among owners and top-level executives morphs into their directing their own operating officers into clandestine meetings, complete with explicit price fixing, bid rigging, and market allocating tactics. Embezzlement of corporate assets starts by helping oneself to unauthorized, one-time bonus payouts. The one-time payout turns into a cumulative sequence of events that then turns into systematic looting. This disregard for legitimate behavior may then open the door to backdating of stock options, lying to compensation committees, money laundering, and attempts to assemble political cover for misdeeds.

In a cumulative sequence of events, criminal routines are integrated into the ordinary occupational and organizational routines of an enterprise. At its most thorough, a cumulative sequence transforms an organization into a weapon of attack. Criminal organization slides along a continuum from partial to total integration of illegal repertoires with the legal repertoires of the company or enterprise. It becomes a constituent feature of the "modus operandi of misdeeds" (Shapiro 1990, 363).

In corporations where financial trust is critical and therefore easily open to abuse, legal and illegal activities may combine loosely or tightly or somewhere in between. The collective repertoires in these production markets reveal the level of "lawlessness" of big companies (Ross 1980), the organization as a "weapon" in white-collar crime (Wheeler and Rothman 1982; Selznick 1960), the abuse and conflicts of interest on Wall Street (Levitt 2002; Twentieth Century Fund 1980), and the role of the state in networks of corruption (Handelman 1995; Rose-Ackerman 1978; Greene 1981).

Several features of these findings and their implications for a theory of accusations in organizations are worth highlighting.

First, accusations are more art than law. Every allegation is tailored to meet the needs of decision-makers, shareholders, and stakeholders. Every allegation we studied is a calibrated series of messages and symbolic gestures that spoke to and about ideas of how things should be done. Each one precedes more formal, legal handling of the putative wrongdoing. Thus, whereas criminological studies strive principally to use legal standards, sociological studies should be dedicated to providing analysis of events, which occur in the so-called "shadow of the law" (Mnookin and Kornhauser 1979). Our view throughout is that the accusation is a resource for revealing the explicit contracts, implicit agreements, and taken-for-granted understandings underlying economic life. An accusation is not a proxy for a crime, nor should it be studied as such. As noted above, it straddles the line between private grievances, murmurings – and informal – recriminations accompanying wrongdoing and the more public – and formal – civil filings of complaints citing violations of law.

Accusations as art are intermediate processes of contestation; they lie between becoming offended and calling the cops. That in-betweenness is the perfect laboratory for the study of the *definition of the situation* in the market. As we have shown, when there is a socially and statistically significant pattern of co-occurrence between market-based ties and principal themes, we have repertoires of (alleged) wrongdoing. This co-occurrence is the result of "communicative processes" in corporate markets. The following remarks can be used to explain how accusations, and the art of the specific reveal the dynamics of principal themes.

"The work of Allport and Postman…is the most comprehensive study of this kind. They summarize their findings in terms of three concepts: leveling, which designates the tendency of accounts to become shorter, more concise, and more easily grasped; sharpening, the tendency toward selective perception, retention and reporting of a limited number of details; and assimilation, the tendency of reports to become more coherent and more consistent with the presuppositions and interests of the subjects… From this standpoint it is not easy to make clear distinction between communicative processes and the product of communication. Rumor content is not viewed as an object to be transmitted but as something that is shaped, reshaped, and reinforced in a succession of communicative acts; as Turner (1964, 398) puts it, rumor is not so much the dissemination of a designated message as the process of forming a definition of a situation" (Shibutani 1966, 5, 9; see also Cicourel 1968, 332–37).

Second, the announcement of an accusation can be an organizational weapon in the struggle for power and advantage among large corporations and a tool in the hands of governments and regimes. Over 50 percent of the cases are accusations brought by the Justice Department, Securities and Exchange Commission, Federal Trade Commission, or other regulatory bodies. In 15 percent of the cases, the accuser is a state department of commerce, division of securities, or a state attorney general. There are over one hundred cases of businesses accusing other businesses of misrepresentation, misdirection, or circumvention. The role of the accuser deserves further study for levels of state resources; fads and fashion in detection and enforcement of white collar and corporate crime, and political regime affect the density of accusations and also the destiny of businesses.

Third, lying, cheating, stealing, and other forms of economic opportunism are not the only kinds of allegations. Obviously, there is a wide range of schemas from treason to heresy to rebellion as well as the well-studied accusatory events such as witchcraft, torture, discrimination, and zealotry. Like studies of modern illegal insider trading associated with merger announcements, looting and embezzlement from the corporation, and colluding with market rivals, these other types of accusations involving social, political, and religious institutions are major units of observation for sociological and political analysis.

Shibutani observes: "Rumors exist only in the communicative acts of men, but they cannot be identified in terms of any particular set of words. What is identified as a 'rumor' is usually a shorthand expression summarizing the general sense of many different verbalizations. A particular message may be stated as an affirmation, or it may be part of a question. It may be a direct statement, or it may be implied in what he said. In each universe of discourse certain things are taken for granted and need not be said at all…"

"The basic unit of analysis becomes the ambiguous situation, and the central problem is to ascertain how working orientations toward it develop. If rumors are viewed as the cooperative improvisation of interpretations, it becomes apparent that they cannot be studied fruitfully apart from the social contexts in which they arise" (Shibutani 1966, 16, 23–24.).

Fourth, timing is of the essence. By designating the announcement date as the *first* Internet news report to identify the name of accused corporation and the accusation of wrongdoing, a tracking of economic consequences can be accomplished. The impact of allegations on stock prices is an obvious consequence. Analysts of insider trading might consider the preannouncement period that ascribes a significant portion of preannouncement gains to legal trading by arbitrageurs, stock analysts, short-traders, and other expert professionals.

As Shibutani notes, "Popular definitions are usually oversimplifications and are often couched in stereotyped terms. In the course of development certain objects and symbols begin to stand out and become the focus of special concern" (Shibutani 1966, 69). As Allport and Postman (1958, 61) stated in their classic study of rumor, "It generally happens that items become sharpened or leveled to fit the leading motif of the story, and they become consistent with this motif in such a way as to make the resulting story more coherent, plausible, and well-rounded." A theme emerges in the careers of these market accusations. The themes are primary and intermediate: primary because misrepresentation, misdirection, and circumvention are the dominant motifs in markets; intermediate because they stand between the weak informal complaints and the strong charges of violations of laws.

For example, in tracing the careers of financial frauds, securities violations, and breach of conduct accusations, the storyline becomes sharpened into a leading motif that results in a "more coherent, plausible, and well-rounded" theme. As an example, in the unfolding and complex set of investment frauds involving Bernard L. Madoff's investment company, Madoff was accused of having misled his clients for nearly a decade and relying on a vast network of money managers and hedge funds managers. These managers were accused of deliberately deceiving clients about their role and ties to Madoff, of charging for services not rendered, and of deceit, recklessness and breaches of fiduciary duty. In the beginning of the career of this fraud, attention was quickly focused on the $65 billion financial fraud characterized as a "Ponzi scheme" (Henriques 2009). Madoff and "Ponzi scheme" were joined, and they became a symbol that elicited unrestrained hostility on the part of others – specifically investors, regulators, hedge fund managers, and the business press. "Thus, in each context certain events and objects come to stand out, and the situation is eventually defined in these terms (Shibutani 1966, 69).

Fifth, what is the market reaction to adverse publicity? What happens to the price of the corporation's stock when an announcement is published in the *Wall Street Journal*? Should a corporation accused of an illegal act expect its stock price to react? What is the reaction of investors and the market to allegations of fraudulent financial reporting, defense contract or other government fraud, defrauding of stakeholders, embezzlement, insider trading, collusion with competitors, and violations of regulations? How does the stock price react to different accusational themes and different market-based ties? Is there a negative stock price reaction (Karpoff and Lott 1993), no reaction (Lukawitz and Steinbart 1995), or perhaps positive reaction to the first accusation story published in the *Wall Street Journal*?

After the passage of the 2002 Sarbanes–Oxley Act, which was intended to hold executives more accountable for their corporations' actions, the Justice Department revisited its Foreign Corrupt Practices Act law as part of the overall crackdown on corporate shenanigans. In 2007 the Justice Department accused the telecommunications company Lucent Technologies Inc. of failing to record properly millions of dollars in bribes to Chinese foreign officials who worked for state-controlled companies. They eventually settled charges against the company, which had booked trips to Las Vegas and Disney World as "factory tours." After taking a hit and sharply declining, Lucent's stock price eventually recovered subsequent to the firm's admission to the bribery and paying a $2.5 million fine.

In 2004 the Justice Department accused, officially probed, and then charged a defense services company, Titan Corp., of overseas bribery, sending its stock on a downward slide; the firm abandoned its $1.6 billion merger with Lockheed Martin Corp., the aerospace giant. In early 2009 lawyers from Sun Microsystems and Oracle Corp. were in the midst of negotiations on a merger, an acquisition deal worth over

$7.4 billion. Sun declared in a regulatory filing that it might be involved in violation of bribery rules and regulations in an unnamed country. The two corporations apparently hired consultants to internally investigate the matter, putting the negotiations on hold. The stock price of both firms was only modestly affected.

Davidson and Worrell (1988) write the following: "[C]ommitting a crime or even getting caught may still not have a negative effect on firm value. Some crimes may be intrinsically bad and may harm society in general... Other crimes may be designated as such because the government has been pressured to so label them; antitrust violations are an example. The stock market may be sensitive to type of illegality." They continue, "Future research should also attempt to take into account the beneficial effects of illegal acts. Ethnical issues aside, from a shareholder's standpoint, illegal acts may be worthwhile if their expected benefits outweigh their expected costs... Some investors may view managerial attempts to test the legal waters as preferable to always proceeding in a risk-averse manner. Wealth-maximizing shareholders may consider it desirable for managers to occasionally get caught trying to cheat." As the saying goes in NASCAR racing circles, "If you are not cheating, you are not trying."

That said, being bad, or being accused of wrongdoing, may usher in a trip to bankruptcy court or even the dissolution of the firm. The corporate landscape is littered with dead firms, from Enron to Lincoln Savings and Loan to Drexel. More recently, in 2009, as his company, Pequot Capital Management – a pioneering, well-connected, and hugely capitalized hedge fund – came under continuing scrutiny, and as its founder, Arthur Samberg, was accused of insider trading in Microsoft Corp. stock, he wrote, "Public disclosures about the continuing investigation have cast a cloud over the firm and have become a source of personal distraction." In late May of 2009, after a couple of years of allegations of trading on proprietary information as well as and rumors about very cozy relations with politicians and federal regulators, it was time to throw in the towel. It was "increasing[ly] untenable for the firm and for me. I have concluded that Pequot can no longer stay in business." Pequot's white-collar executives never committed, nor was the corporation ever charged with, a criminal or civil offense. Moreover, as of May 17, 2009 Pequot was neither formally accused of a crime nor ever served a Wells Notice; the notice is an announcement and formal, public notice that an agency of the government finds a corporation in violation of laws sufficiently serious to open a formal investigation.

Future research is needed to focus on the relationship between dissolution of the corporation and the basis of announcement of the accusation, principal theme and market tie, as well as shareholder returns. The restricted scope of this study suggests that additional research on stock market reactions to accusation types is warranted.

Sixth, we have focused on economic wrongdoing and slighted the theoretical literature and empirical accusations surrounding human rights abuses by corporations, violation of environmental and safety regulations (Gray and Shadbegian 2005), the nature of rules and guidelines concerning the Occupational Safety and Health Administration (OSHA) (Gray and Scholz 1993), and the informal and formal steps in enforcing equal employment opportunity (EEO) law. For example, Title VII of the Civil Rights Act and related EEO laws are generated and enforced primarily through workers' complaints of discrimination. The Civil Rights Act prohibits discrimination in employment, making it unlawful for employers to hire, fire, compensate, classify, or deprive workers of opportunities based on their sex, color, race, religion, or national origin. Many scholars note the limited regulatory scope and capacity of state agencies in general and the Equal Employment Opportunity Commission (EEOC) in particular (Dobbin and Sutton 1998; Edelman 1992; Pedriana and Stryker 2004; Reskin 2001). "The EEOC cannot initiate investigations of discrimination, and it lacks formal enforcement powers beyond the purview of individual complaints. For workers who *do file claims,* the EEOC adjudication process offers modest relief. Of the roughly 60,000 sex and race discrimination claims filed annually with the EEOC, fewer than 1 in 10 are substantiated by EEOC investigators and fewer than 1 in 5 result in benefits – such as monetary payouts or positive changes in workplace conditions – for the complainant..." (Hirsh 2009, emphasis added).

Hirsh describes the winnowing process of moving from private and informal "claims" to public and formal, legal filings. "When the EEOC receives a charge of discrimination, it conducts an investigation of the accused workplace, reviewing employment practices related to the grievance raised in the claim. During investigations, the EEOC requires employers to submit position statements that outline the establishments' side of the story; the EEOC may also request personnel files, payroll records, progress reviews, internal memos, and other documents that could aid investigators in determining a claim's merit. *If* investigators determine that employment practices are in violation of the law (or in circumstances where employers are willing to settle the case to avoid an administrative or legal battle), settlements involving monetary payouts or mandated changes in employment policies typically follow" (Hirsh 2009, 247, emphasis added). Hirsh notes that in her sample, "[R]oughly 14 percent of race charges and 19 percent of sex charges resulted in settlements favorable to the complainant" (Hirsh 2009, 247).

Hirsch continues, "One important byproduct of charges and sanctions is the example they set for others and the opportunity they provide to communicate what constitutes fair and lawful employment practices." Complaints, charges, accusations, and allegations cultivate an external environment that can discourage the sanctioned behavior, whether they be EEO compliance issues, workplace discrimination charges, lawsuits following accusations of violation of air and soil pollution rules, and regulations or individual workplace complaints about systematic occupational safety and health infractions. As institutional theory might point out, a driving force of an accusation is not only the sanctions that can follow, but the cultural environment an allegation creates as firms watch one another and respond to one another's actions as allegations move from the private sphere to the public sphere.

Finally, the dual embeddedness of recipes (culture) and market-based ties (structure) demonstrate the cultural and social "context" in which accusations arise. This context is the market as an "institutionalized mechanism...which facilitates exchange" (Baker, Faulkner, and Fisher 1998, 148) and argues that accusations represent market-based ties gone sour, insomuch as interorganizational relationships are allegations of wrongdoing, contestation, and termination within such institutionalized mechanisms for exchange. Resource dependency theory suggests that interorganizational market ties can lead to undesirable dependence, constraints, and warnings of potential trouble (Pfeffer and Nowak 1976). Relying on external organizations to access vital market resources also entails certain hazards, such as relationship exploitation, resource redundancy, and conflicting interests, which can all contribute to underperformance. Underperformance can lead to finger pointing and charges centering about sub-par market competitiveness rather than potentially criminal conduct.

There are variations on the way contestation over market-based ties become repertoires, and the way buyers, sellers, and regulators use repertoire shows how the workings of the relatively small number of mechanisms and elements we have described can produce highly variable results in the market. Overall, the utility of the concept of cultural repertoire should be explored by focusing on the uses of recipes and routes in other settings. We only examined ideas and actions in economic exchange. The use of recipes as resources in more complex settings should be studied, including the analysis of the emergence of new recipes, with specifications of the conditions and circumstances that foster or impede their emergence in markets. A theory of repertoire should consider more explicitly the role of the state and courts. Because accusations of wrongdoing by businesses occur within a larger legal context, it is important to take into account the influence of local and state rules and codes as well as the influence of case law within federal circuits where allegations of big business crime may be heard.

Also, because our data are restricted to large, heavily capitalized firms, future research might examine accusations in the context of small establishments and public-sector organizations. In such contexts, the process by which accusations are aired might take place informally and without the threat of regulatory enforcement. Even for small establishments that are, of course, subject to laws governing fraud, insider trading, collusion, and false filing, norms of informality and personal contact might discourage personnel and regulators from bring formal accusations and claims. Thus, in restricting the analysis to private, publicly traded firms, we cannot observe how the process of identifying and claiming economic wrongdoing might vary between public and private establishments.

Nor did we focus on political organizations such as the Republican or Democratic reelection campaign organizations. Recent allegations of theft from the National Republican Congressional Committee (NRCC) highlights the embarrassing and painful consequences experienced when federal prosecutors accuse top-level treasurers of fabricating statements to hide missing money. "We have been deceived and betrayed for a number of years by a highly respected and trusted individual," said one representative and chairman of the NRCC, who added that a criminal investigation was ongoing into the now former treasurer's submission of fake audit reports, redirecting funds into his own bank account, and using the stolen money to remodel and pay the mortgage on his home.

In addition, we did not focus on commodities futures market and the roles played by speculators and traders. The commodity market has seen its share of manipulation scandals – allegations that the Hunt family of Texas had manipulated the silver market in 1979, allegations that executives at the J.R. Simplot firm had attempted to fix the Maine potato market in 1976, and in 2007, BP's settlement of federal charges that it had manipulated propane prices.

Our examination of accusations in markets of large-cap corporations shows how the United States government, usually regarded as a passive or weak state, exercises considerable influence on the economy by defining the scope and depth of the recipe we called "circumvention." All states are not the same. Some have elaborate regulations, sets of ministries and regulative agencies that assume extensive responsibility for supervising and directing the affairs of economic markets. Other states have less elaborate regulations and fewer sets of agencies that undertake directive action into the market. Some states are disposed to manage the market; others are disposed to merely provide a framework for the economy.

Comparative studies of accusations and globalization are needed. Changing rules of market conduct vary across the globe. Bribery, for example, definitively became a crime in Germany only in 2004. The country adopted the Anti-Bribery Convention established by the Organization for Economic Cooperation and Development (OECD); until then, bribery could be defined as a business cost and placed under the rubric of "useful expenditures." Firms such as Siemens, the German industrial giant, and MAN, the German truck maker and one of the biggest industrial companies in the country, instituted stricter codes of conduct and developed procedures to encourage white-collar and blue-collar employees to report breaches of proper business conduct. After this scandal, in which the firm was changed with the biggest bribery scandal in business history, MAN appointed a staff of ombudsmen to vet accusations from whistle-blowers inside the firm and investigate potential violations of corporate standards. Comparative studies of misrepresentation, misdirection, and circumvention in Europe, Asia, and the Middle East would reveal important intersections between law, the state, regulators, corporations, and changes in rules as well as different styles of framing key words in accusational activity. The strange history of insider trading rules and regulations in our own country offers a challenging local study; the emergence of the Foreign Corrupt Practices Act in the wake of Watergate offers another. The two faces of accusation offer possibilities for investigators the world over.

The methods for organizing government affect the recipes of circumvention as well as the recipes of misrepresentation and redirection. The US Supreme Court has recently refused standing to large numbers of litigants as accusers to challenge corporate actions. The court reduced the possibility of punitive damages, cut back regulatory agencies' powers, and reached out for cases to be decided in a pro-business way, acknowledging its commitment, some say, to as free a market as possible with as little regulation as possible. The impact of the court's decisions on affecting the sum total of accusations in an organizational field of companies would be a useful line of inquiry for the study of law and society.

The stage in the career of an accusation is crucial. The allegation of opportunistic exploitation makes its way from initial accusation to criminal investigation to formal charges, conviction, presentencing decisions, and final disposition. Criminal indictments can destroy entire corporations, as seen in the case of Arthur Andersen, the accounting firm that closed down in 2002 after being indicted in the Enron scandal. Drexel Burnham Lambert's meltdown and filing for bankruptcy in February of 1990 began with initial, and very tentative, allegations of stock parking, accounting trickery, and associated shenanigans of the junk-bond-backed debt binge that Drexel and its leader, Michael Milken, engineered (Siconolfi et al. 1990).

In the last few years, the Justice Department has used so-called "deferred prosecutions" to get companies accused of wrongdoing to pay fines and change their internal practices without being formally charged. In cases involving Bristol-Myers Squibb, for example, a corporate monitor is brought in to check on the firm's compliance with department directives and ensure progress in living up to its promises of internal change. Nonprosecution agreements represent, as an informant noted, "the middle ground" between suspicions of corporate impropriety and not bringing a criminal prosecution on the one hand, and formally charging the company with criminal action on the other.

Accusations are at the intersection of social control and the moral order. In the context of small groups, Whyte (1943, 257) found that an underlying "system of mutual obligations" was "fundamental" to group cohesion of the "corner boys," noting that "it is only when the relationship breaks down that the underlying obligations are brought to light." The squawk in small groups and economic transactions allows us to explore the intersection between accusation and opportunism, facilitating a more precise understanding of both mutual obligations and wrongdoing in markets. If, as we have suggested, the spread of opportunism and unsavory business practices represents a threat to the viability of economic markets, then we must identify the precise types of accusations of wrongdoing and the precise routes and mechanisms that bring them to light.

Key phrases, keywords, and accusation themes as repertoires need to be examined, expanded, and refined in other institutional settings, notably the world of political campaigns, the antiques business, the criminal justice system, the military, church, the medical profession, and science. The political and economic consequences of allegations of faking, theft, dishonesty, dissemblance and exploitation in institutions have societal-wide implications. The triad of state–market–firm revealed in allegations is a powerful resource for those working in the scholarly fields of economic sociology, political economy, criminology, and social theory.

All of us would like to believe in a just world. All of us would like to believe in open, transparent, and fair markets. Capitalism isn't perfect. Indeed, to paraphrase Winston Churchill's famous description of democracy, it's the worst economic system except for all the others. But the inescapable fact is that in real markets (rather than abstract "market forces"), opportunism is a persistent and durable feature of economic behavior. In the corporate world there are repeat offenders with accusations against them that suggest deception and audacity on an extraordinary scale. The scandals at Enron, WorldCom, Tyco, Ameriquest, American International Group, Equity Funding, Lincoln Savings and Loan, Citigroup, Archer Daniels Midland, Boeing, Exxon, Pfizer, and MiniScribe, to mention a few high-profile cases, *all began* with Washington and/or state regulators, industry suppliers, customers, or competitive rivals accusing them of wrongdoing. In the aftermath of the postmillennial corporate scandals, regulators, investors, analysts, auditors, and academics have agreed that markets are far from ideal. Unfortunately, economic sociologists do not agree on what it means to speak of markets as networks or cultures and seldom address the phenomenon of crime in and around markets.

Sociological studies of economic transactions have shown that exchanges are colored by both market and nonmarket considerations (Bradach and Eccles 1989; Granovetter 1985). Organizational exchanges are also colored by both normative and nonnormative actions and reactions. With these large-cap corporations, our empirical analysis also implies that both legal and potentially illegal considerations provide key insights into understanding where accusations over deceptive pricing, misuse of authority roles, conspiracy to restrain trade, and violations of trust are embedded in market transactions.

As we noted at the outset, because accusations are such an important part of organizations in markets, reaching a thorough understanding of them is essential for theories of socioeconomic behavior. The study of behavior against markets as a substantive topic *and* analytic program for economic sociology has a long way to go. Regardless of the specific mechanisms investigated, further progress in economic sociology depends upon enlarging our vision. Modern finance theory is based on the notion that markets are ever efficient. This means that exchanges result in correctly priced goods. Scholars have based their careers on this doctrine. Perhaps they see repertoires of wrongdoing as a challenge to the doctrine of legal markets. Some industrial economists and economic sociologists have described malfeasance and wrongdoing in markets as a "black box," undeserving of study, or at best left to the sociology of law or criminology. It is time to watch crime in markets as an observable phenomenon, for socioeconomic actors do watch one another's behavior and develop responses and roles from what they observe.

It is clear from this, then, that in explaining any institution, it cannot be merely assumed that accusations of wrongdoing will operate in any given case, but it is necessary to establish empirically both their occurrence and their institutionally based ties. Instead of focusing on institutional prescriptions of unconstrained "generosity," such as the Christian notion of "turning the other cheek," the feudal concept of noblesse oblige, the Roman notion of "clemency," or the industrial mechanisms of "indulgency," we have examined the seamy side of an institution. We have focused on critical situations in between informal complaints and formal criminal charges, the finger pointing, allegation making, and striking back rather than letting it pass. These highly charged actions and reactions enable sociologists to address the significance of the strength of moral obligations in institutions. The keywords, and the key phrases of wrongdoing are signs not of the moral decay, but of moral ferment.

But perhaps, if the reader is of an artistic bent, you might conclude that accusations are like absinthe, the devil's glamour drink, so disreputable, so interesting, so confusing, so louche. Oscar Wilde said of the green torment, "After the first glass, you see things as you wish they were. After the second, you see things as they are not. Finally, you see things as they really are, and that is the most horrible thing in the world."

Appendix A
Notes on Statistical Analysis and Coding Principal Themes, Keywords, and Key Phrases in the Accusations

In the quantitative analysis of the co-occurrence of themes and market-based ties, we employed two statistical methods: (1) traditional cross-tabular analysis, including chi-square tests of the significance of the frequency and percent distributions of wrongdoing by ideas or templates (recipes) and enactments or exchange paths (routes); and (2) a log-linear analysis to test the significance of the interaction effect of recipes and routes on the frequencies of accusation. A regression-based approach to the log-linear analysis (Anderton and Cheney 2004; Long 1997; Powers and Xie 2000) is specified as:

$$\text{Log (frequency of accusation)} = B1Xi1 + B2Xi2$$
$$= \ldots + BkXik + ei$$

Variables in the above equation are indicator variables representing each recipe, route, and the interaction effects of ideas and actions (i.e., the joint occurrence of a recipe and route). Coefficients in the equation in Table 3 represent the effect of each recipe, route, and their interactions on the frequencies of accusations.

We estimated the regression model using a Poisson model. Poisson models do not assume linearity in the dependent variable and are thus suitable for nominal-level data, and the long-linear analysis allows for the statistical test of each recipe, route, and their interactive effects.

We also employed Wald test statistics to assess the individual coefficients and derived odds ratios on the rates of accusations. We used likelihood ratio and Poisson goodness-of-fit chi-squared test statistics to test the contribution of recipes, routes, and the interactions on the frequencies of accusations. With routes and recipes properly specified, the effects are positive and highly significant.

A note on coding accusations attached to a corporation over time. A team of coders read every word of every newspaper article in which a corporation was linked to an accusation. They noted the time at which the first accusation appeared, the level of publicity the corporation received, the time at which subsequent accusation events occurred, whether the article appeared on page 1 or the front of the business section of a major newspaper (*New York Times, Wall Street Journal*), and the total number of articles devoted to covering the accusation linked to the firm over the study period. A count of column inches was compiled. And we also paid attention to the ordering of the accusation by firm data as repeated or recurrent event data, where the company may experience the same event multiple times during the follow-up period after the initial or first accusation.

Recurrent accusation and column level data are a special type of event history information. They record the depth of coverage and the timing of transitions between two or more accusation events. Event "risk" process of later accusations can depend on the previous history of the event process and we wanted to pay attention to the career the accused corporation as it unfolded over time. We find that high-risk or "frail" corporations tend to experience accusations (1) early in the event process, (2) on paths 1, 2, and 4, and (3) with a hazard rate decreasing over time. This problem is referred to as spurious duration dependence in the statistical literature (Ezell, Land, Cohen 2003; Heckman and Singer 1984). A separate analysis of these accusations as corporate failures and their timing and occurrence in markets is provided elsewhere (Faulkner 2009).

In coding Internet archives, a matrix was constructed for each firm: three possible recipes and six possible routes. If the accusations were for a combination of "embezzlement, looting, and theft from the firm," for example, we coded this as an instance of stealing from the firm

(A1, n = 110). If the set was stealing confidential and proprietary information and passing that information on to someone who knew that it was insider information, we coded this as insider trading (C1, n = 127). Multiple allegations of an intra-industry conspiracy, price-fixing schemes, and restraint of trade were counted as a single accusation type or event (C2, n = 157).

Table 2 lists the 18 possible combinations. Three coders and the author independently coded the content of the accusations against corporations; inter-rater reliability was robust (.86). Collapsing the possible array of accusations into a single type of occurrence may understate the frequency of occurrences. Even in the small set of situations where the accusation profile is heterogeneous the events composing the dominant accusation type are usually highly correlated.

In the case of collusion, we recognize that the conspiracy may have involved many overt actions in furtherance of the scheme and may have involved many transactions with several buyers or bidders. Multiple firms were accused of being involved in the price fixing and were coded as such. Similarly, accusations of swindling or misrepresentation involving many clients and customers (A4) may also involve repeated transactions and were coded as a single occurrence. There were 61 cases. Accusations of obstruction of justice (C6) are the lead allegation. There are 25 cases that can also involve perjury and occasionally destruction of documents. For a similar logic in the coding of white-collar crime data, see Wheeler and Rothman (1982, 1410n26). Wheeler and Rothman's data are drawn from presentence investigation reports (PSIs) for persons *convicted* of eight white-collar crimes prosecuted in federal courts (Wheeler and Rothman 1982: 1406). Clinard and Yeager (1980) focus on corporations *formally charged* with administrative violations.

Recall coding of the accusation is about the earliest announcement of an accusation, occurring before the informal inquiries commence, the formal investigation gets started, before the subpoenas arrive, before the charges are handed down, and before the "perp walks" are taken, the convictions announced, the presentence reports filed, and the criminal sentence handed down.

Interviews with division of securities staff inform the coding of initial accusation rather than the formally charged administrative or criminal violation. "It takes a long time to investigate cases," said one of the lawyers we talked to. There could be many explanations for the absence of criminal charges after the accusation is made (and coded according to our protocol): The federal and state authorities could still be investigating; they could have "high suspicion" of an economic crime but insufficient proof; or the allegations could simply be false. And, one lawyer noted, the statute of limitations could expire.

The coding focuses on a *specific* set of economic (alleged) crimes. We exclude accusations concerning the following allegations: those concerning environmental and "green" violations, Equal Employment Opportunity violations, and workplace and institutional environment claims of sex and race discrimination. Nor do we focus on hate crimes in corporations, whistle-blower charges and other disputes unrelated to economic crimes, and accusations of violations of federal workplace, occupational, health, and safety rules. A primary selection criterion for defining an accusation of economic crime was whether the event was mentioned as an accusation or allegation in the Internet archive/newspaper sources used. Some of these events lasted over long periods of time, but these were each coded as a single accusation event to avoid data inflation.

To control for problems with selection and description bias, newspaper accounts were triangulated with other sources. By triangulating news sources with state departments of commerce (i.e., divisions of securities), Securities and Exchange Commission filings, or other electronic media sources, we garnered a broader coverage of events, and included multiple accounts of the same accusations over time to check for possible bias in their reporting. The "hard news" of accusations reported in Internet archives such as LexisNexis appears to be accurate and reliable for the purposes of this study.

The research described in this book is not designed primarily to unravel the consequences of accusations in the criminal justice system. Criminologists may be tempted to complain that by studying allegations we are not studying crime. As noted, earlier, they might say that we are not properly measuring the criminal and legal content of the events charged against a corporation: they are "mere accusations." They may claim that anonymous sources are making the complaints, that the complaints are too early in the legal process, and that accusations are trivial, unreliable, and fictitious – in effect, mere accusations.

Unfortunately, this view does not square with our knowledge of social theory. Recall that contending parties were considering their interests not only in narrow criminal justice terms but also in the context of market norms. Someone is taking umbrage, and that someone is a specific regulator, supplier, customer, or client who is offended by the market behavior of someone else. We prefer emphasizing how complaints and accusations tap into those consensual attachments to norms. Our quantitative data and qualitative stories of wrongdoing indicate that accusations as social events are serious occurrences where one party "goes public" and stakes a claim. If there is an important role for socioeconomic norms (norms shared by the vast majority of market players) in criminal law, that role may have as much to with the *processes* by which an accusation is initially made and the institutions in which those processes occur, as it has to do with the *content* of the eventual criminal-legal decision. In addition to counting column inches of accusation coverage, we count quotations and statements from the accuser and assert that these clearly are official statements that an institution and its actors are standing behind, whether the institution is the Justice Department or the Federal Trade Commission, and the actors are investigators for a state attorney general, the head of a state department of commerce, lawyers for the Securities and Exchange Commission, or executives of large-cap corporations.

Finally, the focus on American firms and economic behavior in the quantitative analysis excludes decades of accusation and investigation into corporate bribery, fraud, and corruption in Britain, Germany, France, Canada, and Japan. A recent survey published by Integrity Interactive found that economic crimes such as bribery, corrupt foreign payments, and ethnics involving "commissions" have become a great concern among to the heads of legal departments and compliance offices at one hundred of Europe's largest corporations (Clark 2008).

Appendix B
A Sample of United States Corporations and Counts of Public Announcements of Alleged Economic Crime – 1994 (fourth quarter) to 2006 (first quarter)

No. of corporations in sample = 427
Total no. of public announcements of alleged economic crime = 1,103

Amoco Oil Co. 4
AMP Inc. 0
AMPCO-Pittsburg Corp. 0
Anacomp, Inc. 2
Aaron Rents 2
Abbot Laboratories 10
Addison-Wesley Pub. 0
Advanced Micro Devices 13
Advanced Systems, Inc. 0
Advest Group 0
Aetna Life & Casualty 10
Ahmanson (H.F.) & Co. 1
Air Products & Chemicals, Inc. 2
Alexander & Baldwin 1
Allen Group 0
Allied Signal Inc. 4

Aluminum Co. of America 0
Amax, Inc. 2
American Airlines Inc. 10
American Brands 3
American Broadcasting Co., Inc. 0
American Cyanamid Co. 0
American Electric Power 6
American Express 12
American General Corp. 3
American Home Products 15
American Honda Motor Co. 6
American Information Technologies 0
American International Group 14
American Maize-Products 0
American Medical Services 0
American Motors Corp. 0

American Standard, Inc. 5
American Telephone and Telegraph 11
Anchor Hocking Corp. 0
Anderson, Clayton & Co. 0
Anheuser-Busch Co. 14
Anixter Bros. 0
Anthony Industries, Inc.
Argosystems, Inc. 1
Artra Group, Inc. 0
Arvin Industries, Inc. 0
Atlantic Richfield Co. 10
Avery International 0
Avnet, Inc. 0
Avon Products 3

Bally Manufacturing Corp. 0
Bandag, Inc. 0
Basic American Medical, Inc. 1
Bassett Furniture Industries 0
Batus, Inc. 0
Bausch & Lomb, Inc. 4
BayBanks, Inc. 4
Beatrice Companies, Inc. 2
Beecham Products Div. 0
Bell Atlantic Corp. 13
Bell Industries, Inc. 0
Bell South Corp. 0
Bemis Co. 0
Bethlehem Steel Corp. 3
Big Y Super Markets 0
Bio-Rad Laboratories 2
Boeing Co. 22
Borg-Warner Corp. 3
Bristol-Meyers Co. 3
Brown Group, Inc. 0
Brown-Forman, Inc. 0
Burlington Northern 5

CBS Inc. 9
CNA Financial Corp. 5
CPC International Inc. 3
CSX Corp. 2
Callahan Mining Corp.
Camco Inc. 2
Campbell Soup Co. 1
Canon U.S.A. 0

Caremark 8
Carnation Co./subs of Nestlé 4
Carpenter Technology 6
Caterpillar, Inc. 5
Celanese Corp. 3
Cenergy Corp. 0
Centronics Data Computer 0
Cetus Corp. 0
Champion Home
      Builders Co. 0
Chesebrough-Pond's Inc. 0
Chevron Corp. 15
Chrysler Corp. 5
Cigna Corp. 17
Circuit City Stores, Inc. 0
Citicorp/Citigroup 10
Clayton Homes Inc. 1
Cleveland-Cliffs Inc. 0
Clorox Company 1
Coca-Cola Co. 12
Coleco Industries Inc. 0
Colonial Life and Accident 2
Combustion Engineering, Inc. 1
Commerce Bancshares, Inc. 7
Commercial Metals Co. 0
Commonwealth Edison 0
Commonwealth Tel.
      Enterprises 0
Consolidated Edison 3
Consolidated Foods Co. 1
Continental Airlines Corp. 3
Continental Corp. 0
Coopervision, Inc. 1
Coors, Adolph, Co. 3
Corning Glass Works 0
Cosmair, Inc. 0
Culbro Corp. 3

DSC Communications Corp. 0
Daniel Industries 2
Dart & Kraft, Inc. 0
Data I/O Corp. 0
Dayco Corp. 1
Dayton-Hudson Corp. 2
Dean Foods Co. 4
Dekalb Corporation 0

Delta Airlines 10
Dennison Manufacturing 0
Detroit Edison 0
DiGiorgio Corp. 1
Digital Equipment 3
Disney (Walt) Co. 4
Donaldson Co. 0
Dow Chemical 8
Dravo Corp. 3
Dreyfus Corp. 7
DuPont (E.I.) 12
Dun & Bradstreet Corp. 9

Easter Airlines 0
Eastern Gas & Fuel Association 0
Eastman Kodak Co. 1
Edwards (A.G.), Inc. 6
El Paso Electric Co. 2
Eldon Industries Inc. 0
Electro Catheter Corp. 0
Emerson Electric Co. 5
Emulex Corp. 1
Eqifax, Inc. 1
Exxon Corp. 20

FPL Group, Inc. 3
Fairchild Industries, Inc. 4
Fairfield Communities, Inc. 0
Federal Paper Board Co. 0
Federal Signal Corp. 0
Federated Dept. Stores Inc. 0
Fieldcrest Cannon, Inc. 0
Figgie Intl. Holdings-CLB 0
First Bank System 1
First Maryland Bancorp. 0
First Pennsylvania Corp. 0
Firstcorp., Inc. 1
Fleming Companies Inc. 5
Florida National Banks of
        Florida 1
Fluocarbon Co. 0
Foote Mineral Co. 0
Ford Motor Co. 20
Foxboro Co. 0
Fruehauf Corp. 0
Fur Vault, Inc. 0

GCA Corp. 4
GTE Corp. 2
Gannett Co. 5
General Dynamics Corp. 2
General Electric Co. 5
General Instrument Corp. 0
General Motors Corp. 7
General Pubic Utilities 0
General Re Corp. 4
Genuine Parts Co. 2
Getty Petroleum Corp. 3
Gillette Co. 16
Goodrich (B.F.) Co. 1
Goodyear Tire and Rubber Co. 16
Gordon Jewelry Corp. 0
Grand Auto, Inc. 0
Grandmet U.S.A. Inc. 0
Green Mountain Power Corp. 0
Greyhound Corp. 3

Hall (Frank B.) & Co. 5
Halliburton Co. 6
Hamilton Oil Corp. 0
Handy & Harman 1
Handyman Corp. 0
Harris Corp. 6
Hasbro, Inc. 7
Hecia Mining Co. 0
Heinz (H.J.) Co. 4
Helene Curtis Industries 0
Heritage Communications, Inc. 0
Hershey Foods Corp. 0
Hewlett-Packard Co. 9
Hexcel Corp. 0
Hollywood Park Realty Enterprises 0
Home Depot, Inc. 5
Home Federal S&L Association 1
Horn & Hordart Co.
Howell Corp. 0
Hughes Tool Co. 2

IC Industries, Inc. 0
ITT Corp. 13
Idaho Power Co. 1
Indiana National Corp. 0
Integrated Resources, Inc. 1

Inter-regional Financial Group 3
Interco Inc. 0
International Business Machine 0
International Paper Co. 0
Interpublic Group of Cos. 0

Jerrico. Inc. 1
Johnson & Johnson 4
Jones Intercable Inc. 0
Jorgensen (Earle M.) Co. 0

K Mart Corp. 5
KLA Instruments Corp. 0
Kaiser Cement Corp. 0
Kaufman & Broad Inc. 0
Kay Jewelers Inc. 0
Kellogg Co. 2
Kemper Corp. 4
Kimball International, Inc. 0
Kimberly-Clark Corp. 2
Koppers Co. 0
Kroger Co. 2

La-Z-Boy Chair Co. 0
LaMaur Inc. 0
Ladd Furniture Inc. 0
Landmark Land Co. 2
Lear Siegler Inc. 0
Leaseway Transportation Corp. 0
Lee Data Corp. 0
Lehigh Press Inc. 0
Lever Brothers Co. (subs of
Unilever) 0
Levi Strauss 4
Libbey Owens Ford Co. 3
Liberty Corp. 0
Lilly (Eli) & Co. 5
Limited, Inc. 4
Lin Broadcasting 0
Little (Arthur D.), Inc. 0
Liz Claiborne, Inc. 0
Loews Corp. 5
Lorimar 4
Louisiana General Services 0
Luby's Cafeterias, Inc. 0

MCA 2
MacGregor Sporting Goods, Inc. 0
Magma Power Co. 0
Manhattan Industries, Inc. 0
Marine Corp-Wisconsin 0
Marine Midland Banks 4
Marion Laboratories 3
Mars, Inc. 1
Martin Marietta Corp. 0
Matrix Corp. 0
Mattel, Inc. 4
Maytag Co. 0
Mazda Motors of America, Inc. 0
McDonald's Corp. 3
McLean Industries, Inc. 0
Medtronic, Inc. 4
Mercantile Bancorporation 0
Mercantile Stores Co, Inc. 0
Merck & Co. 9
Midland-Ross Corp. 0
Midlantic Banks, Inc. 1
Miles Laboratories, Inc. 0
Miniscribe Corp. 17
Minnesota Mining and Manufacturing
Company 1
Mobil Corp. 16
Monfort of Colorado, Inc. 0
Montsanto Co. 1
Moore Financial Group Inc. 0
Morgan (J.P.) & Co. 14
Mortgage Growth Investors 0
Moseley Holding Corp. 0
Mosinee Paper Corp. 0
Motorola, Inc. 10
Murray Ohio Manufacturing 0

NCR Corp. 2
NYNEX Corp. 10
National City Corp. 3
Nestle Co., Inc. 3
Nevada Savings & Loan Assoc. 0
New England Electric System 0
New Process Co. 0
New York State Electric & Gas 0
Newmont Mining Corp. 0
Nicolet Instrument 0

Nike 9
Nissan Motors Corp., USA 2
Norfold Southern Corp. 0
Northwest Natural Gas Co. 0
Noxell Corp. 0

Oak Industries Inc. 4
Orion Pictures Corp. 4
Oshkosh B'Gosh Inc. 1
Owens-Corning Fiberglass 0
Oxford Industries, Inc. 0

Pacific Gas & Electric 6
Pacific Telesis Group 0
Paine Webber Group 6
Paradyne Corp. 4
Park-Ohio Industries 0
Penn Virginia Corp. 0
Penney (J.C.) Co. 1
PepsiCo, Inc. 4
Pfizer, Inc. 18
Philip Morris Cos. Inc. 4
Phillips Petroleum Co. 5
Pillsbury Co. 6
Pioneer Standard Electronics 0
Plenum Publishing Corp. 0
Porta Systems Corp. 0
Potlatch Corp. 0
Pratt & Lambert Inc. 0
Price Co. 0
Procter & Gamble Co. 7
Protective Life Corp. 0
Public Service Co of Ind. 0

Questar Corp. 0

RCA Corp. 5
RJR Nabisco, Inc. 14
RTE Corp/Cooper. 0
Radiation Systems, Inc. 0
Radice Corp. 0
Ralston Purina Co. 5
Ramada Inc./Taj 1
Ransburg Electro-Coating Corp. 0
Raytheon Co. 8

Redken Laboratories 1
Reebok International Ltd 9
Regency Electronics 0
Republic Bank Dallas East 0
Resorts International 3
Revere Cooper & Brass, Inc. 0
Revlon, Inc. 3
Roadway Services, Inc. 3
Rockwell International 4
Rowan Companies, Inc. 0
Rubbermaid, Inc. 3

Safeway Stores, Inc. 7
Salomon, Inc. 1
Santa Anita Realty Enterprise 1
Santa Fe Southern Pacific 1
Sargent-Welch Scientific 0
Savin Business Machines Corp. 0
Scan-Tron Corp. 0
Schering-Plough Corp. 6
Schlumberger Ltd 1
Seagram, Joseph E. & Sons, Inc. 4
Sealed Air Corp. 1
Sears, Roebuck & Co. 13
Seton Co. 0
Seven Oaks International, Inc. 0
Shaklee Corp. 0
Showboat, Inc. 0
Sigma-Aldrich/Sigma Instruments 0
Sikes Corp. 0
Smithkline Beckman Corp. 3
Smucker (J.M.) Co. 0
Snap-On Tools Corp. 4
Sony Corp. of America 0
South Carolina National Corp. 0
Southeastern Public Service Co. 1
Southern California Edison 6
Southern Co. 9
Southwestern Bell Co. 2
Sprint/GTE 10
Squibb Corp. 3
Standard Oil Co., Ohio 2
Standard Shares, Inc. 0
Stanhome, Inc. 1
Sterling Drug, Inc. 1
Sterling Software, Inc.

Stone Container Corp. 1
Stop & Shop Companies. 4
Stroh Brewery Co. 0
Sturm, Ruger & Co., Inc. 3
Sun Co. 1
Sysco Corp. 1

Talley Industries 1
Tandem Computers, Inc. 3
Tandon Corp. 0
Tandy Corp. 2
Teledyne, Inc. 4
Tennant Co. 0
Tenneco, Inc. 0
Texaco, Inc. 3
Texas Instruments 0
Texas Utilities 0
Textron, Inc. 1
Thermo Electron Corp. 0
Thomas Industries, Inc. 0
Thousand Trails, Inc. 0
Time Inc. 3
Time Warner 2
Times Mirror Co. 0
Tonka Corp. 1
Tootsie Roll Industries, Inc. 0
Toyota Motor Sales U.S.A., Inc. 2
Transco Energy Co. 3
Transworld Corp. 0
Travelers Corp. 0

U.S. Surgical Corp. 0
U.S. Trust Corp. 5
U.S. West, Inc. 5
UNC, Inc. United Nuclear Corp. 0
Unifirst Corp. 0
Union Carbide Corp. 3
Union Pacific Corp. 0
United Airlines 5

United Inns Inc. 0
United Technologies Corp. 2
United Telecommunications 0
Universal Foods Corp. 1
Universal Leaf Tobacco 0
Upjohn Co. 8

Veeco Instruments 1
Viacom International 1
Volkswagen of America, Inc. 0

Wainoco Oil Corp. 0
Wal-Mart Stores 5
Warner-Lambert Co. 3
Washington Energy Co. 0
Washington REIT 0
Waste Management, Inc. 13
Watkins-Johnson 0
Wedtech Corp. 1
Wendy's International, Inc. 0
Western Savings & Loan
    Association 0
Westinghouse Electric Corp. 9
Weyerhaeuser Co. 2
Wickes Companies, Inc. 0
Wisconsin Public Service 0
Wm. Wrigley Jr. Co. 0
Worthington Industries 0
Wrather Corp. 0

Xerox Corp. 6

Yellow Freight System 0

Zapata Corp. 1
Zero Corp. 0
Zondervan Corp. 0
Zycad Corp. 0

Tables

Table 1. Keywords in Context

Principal Themes (A, B, and C) with Market-Based Ties (Nos. 1–6)			
Market-Based Ties	Principal Theme A: Fraud, Theft, and Duplicity or Deliberate Misrepresentation in Business Transactions	Principal Theme B: Bribery, Extortion, Hostage Taking or Deliberate Misdirection and Misuse of corporate resources	Principal Theme C: Violation of Administrative Rules, Government Regulations, and Circumvention of Securities Law
1. Firm as Victim	Stealing = theft from the firm, embezzlement, and violation of trust or abuse of official corporate role for personal gain. Fraud against the corporation.	Bribing = transaction bribery, quid pro quo dealing, secret inducements.	Trading = insider trading violations and misappropriation of material, nonpublic (proprietary) information and trading on that information.
2. Competitors and Industry Peers	Subterfuge = deliberate damage to business rivals, stealing proprietary information (about costs and pricing policies), theft of rival's research and development secrets, dissemination of misinformation. Sabotage of a rival company's product in development or in the market.	Extorting = predatory pricing, hostage taking, upstream play-to-play schemes, threats of holdup, and extortion.	Colluding = price fixing, market allocation, swapping market information, and secretly administered price; predatory pricing against rivals.
3. Suppliers	Leveraging = theft and misappropriation involving suppliers, vendors, and providers of professional services. Fraud by the firm with suppliers and vendors as the victims.	Rigging = bid manipulation, market reallocation, reciprocal favors and gifts with vendors, downstream pay-to-play schemes with providers of professional services and other suppliers.	Evading = avoiding import quotas, supply-side royalty payments, channel steering involving vendors, suppliers, and providers of professional services.

4. Customers and Clients	Dissembling = "Ponzi schemes," investment hoaxes, hoodwinking or deliberately misleading buyers of products, securities, and services. Knowingly selling defective products and billing customers for payments for those products (and associated services); making false cost estimates. For example, falsifying test data on parts and products sold to commercial companies (aerospace industry) and to the Department of Defense.	Steering = transaction bribery, speed, extortion, coaxing and channel stuffing.	Inflating = exporting, channel stuffing, buyer-side deals, phony inventories, illegal tying arrangements involving automakers, computer companies and the electronics industry. For example, services companies allege that the firm acts illegally in refusing to sell replacement parts of it products, "tying" the sale of service to the sale of parts.
5. Investment Analysts and Raters	Tailoring = opportunistic touting, exaggerated reports and evaluations. Fraud against analysts and industry securities raters.	Spinning = hyper-reciprocity, bribery, and quid pro quo exchanges between parties. Spinning of hot IPO shares occurs when an investment bank offers shares to the executives of a newly public company at extra-low prices in exchange for future underwriting business from the company.	Aiding = avoiding fiduciary obligations, abetting and credentialing phony deals.
6. Government	Filing and securities fraud = false disclosures, fictitious compliance, "smoothing" of quarterly earnings, parking money, faking reserves and other information in official filings.	Greasing = reciprocal dealing with government officials and agents, variance bribery, deal making, secret dealings and business arrangements with federal, state, and local regulators, exclusionary contracts tacitly approved by officials, and improper payments made to foreign party officials and their agents.	Obstructing = obstruction of justice, perjury, destroying documents, and stonewalling.

Table 2. The Accusational Repertoire: The Co-occurrence of Principal Themes, Market-Based Ties, and Keywords for a Sample of American Corporations (1999–2006)

Routes		A: Misrepresentation	B: Misdirection	C: Circumvention	Total
1. Corporation	Illustrative Keyword	*Stealing*	*Bribing*	*Trading*	
	Sample no.	110	11	127	248
	Row %	44.36%	4.44%	51.21%	100%
	Column %	20.26%	8.94%	8.94%	22.48%
2. Rivals	Illustrative Keyword	*Subterfuge*	*Extorting*	*Colluding*	
	Sample no.	48	5	157	210
	Row %	22.86%	2.38%	74.75%	100%
	Column %	8.84%	4.07%	35.93%	19.04%
3. Suppliers	Illustrative Keyword	*Leveraging*	*Rigging*	*Evading*	
	Sample no.	39	18	28	85
	Row %	45.88%	21.28%	32.94%	100%
	Column %	7.18%	14.63%	6.41%	7.71%
4. Buyers	Illustrative Keyword	*Dissembling*	*Steering*	*Inflating*	
	Sample no.	261	44	84	389
	Row %	67.10%	11.31%	21.59%	100%
	Column %	48.07%	35.77%	19.22%	35.27%
5. Investment Community	Illustrative Keyword	*Tailoring*	*Spinning*	*Aiding*	
	Sample no.	21	12	16	49
	Row %	42.86%	24.49%	32.65%	100%
	Column %	3.87%	9.76%	3.66%	4.44%
6. Government	Illustrative Keyword	*Filing*	*Greasing*	*Obstructing*	
	Sample no.	64	33	25	122
	Row %	52.46%	27.05%	20.49%	100%
	Column %	11.79%	26.83%	5.72%	11.06%
Total no. of Keywords in Column		543	123	437	1,103
		49.23%	11.15%	39.62%	100%

Table 2 (*Continued*).   Poisson Goodness of Fit and Incremental Log-Likelihood Statistics*

Covariate Pattern	Goodness of Fit Likelihood Ratio $X2$	Incremental Likelihood Ratio $X2$
Constant Only	972.824	
Recipes	667.736	305.09[a]
Routes	546.032	426.79[b]
Recipes and Routes	240.945	426.79[c]
Recipes and Routes	240.945	305.09[d]
Recipes, Routes, and Interactions		240.94[e]

Notes: a = comparing with constant only model; b = comparing with constant only model; c = comparing with recipes only; d = comparing with routes only; e = comparing with recipe and routes model.

*All chi-square values are statistically significant at the $p < .0001$ level.

References

Abadinsky, Howard. 2003. *Organized Crime*. Belmont, CA: Wadsworth/Thomson Learning.

Abolafia, M. 1997. *Making Markets*. Cambridge, MA: Harvard University Press.

Adams, James. R. 1990. *The Big Fix: Inside the S & L Scandal: How an Unholy Alliance of Politics and Money Destroyed Americas Banking System*. New York: Wiley.

Adams, Julia. 1996. "Principals and agents, colonialists and company men: the decay of colonial control in the Dutch East Indies." *American Sociological Review* 61: 1228.

Adut, Ari. 2005. "A theory of scandal: Victorians, homosexuality, and the fall of Oscar Wilde." *American Journal of Sociology* 111: 213–48.

Agrawal, Anup, and Tommy Cooper. 2007. "Corporate Governance Consequences of Accounting Scandals: Evidence from Top Management, CFO and Auditor Turnover." (October 2007). Paper presented at 2nd Annual Conference on Empirical Legal Studies. Available at SSRN: http://ssrn.com/abstract=970355 (accessed 23 June 2011).

Allport, Gordon W., and Leo Postman. 1946–47. "An Analysis of Rumor." *Public Opinion Quarterly* 10: 501–14.

———. 1947. *The Psychology of Rumor*. New York: Henry Holt and Co.

———. 1958. "The Basic Psychology of Rumor." In *Readings in Social Psychology*, ed. Eleanor E. Maccoby, Theodore M. Newcomb, and Eugene L. Hartley, 54–65. New York: Henry Holt and Company.

Anderson, Jenny, and Michael J. de la Merced. 2007. "13 Accused of Trading As Insiders." *New York Times*, March 2: A1, C4.

Anderton, D. A., and E. R. Cheney. 2004. "Log-linear analysis." In *Handbook of Data Analysis*, ed. Melissa Hardy and Alan Bryman, 285–306. Thousand Oaks, CA: Sage.

Associated Press. 2007. "Ex-Secretary gets 8-year term in Coca-Cola secrets case." *New York Times*, May 24: C3.

Axelrod, Robert. 1976. *Structure of Decision: The Cognitive Maps of Political Elites*. Princeton: Princeton University Press.

Baker, Wayne E. 1984. "The social structure of a national securities market." *American Journal of Sociology* 89: 775–811.

———. 1990. "Market networks and corporate behavior." *American Journal of Sociology* 96: 589–625

————. 2005. *America's Crisis of Values: Reality and Perception*. Princeton: Princeton University Press.

Baker, Wayne E., and Robert R. Faulkner. 1991. "Role as resource in the Hollywood film industry." *American Journal of Sociology* 97: 279–309.

————. 1993. "The Social Organization of Conspiracy: Illegal Networks in the Electrical Equipment Industry." *American Sociological Review* 58: 837–60.

————. 2003. "Diffusion of Fraud: intermediate economic crime and investor dynamics." *Criminology* 41: 1173–1206.

————. 2004. "Social Networks and Loss of Capital." *Social Networks* 26: 91–111.

————. 2009. "Social Capital, Double Embeddedness, and Mechanisms of Stability and Change." *American Behavioral Scientist* 52: 1531–1555

Baker, Wayne E., Robert R. Faulkner, and Gene A. Fisher. 1998. "Hazards of the market: the continuity and dissolution of interorganizational market relationships." *American Sociological Review* 63: 147–77.

Barney, Jay B., and William G. Ouchi. 1986. *Organizational Economics: Toward a New Paradigm for Understanding and Studying Organizations*. San Francisco: Jossey-Bass.

Bass, Ron, and Lois Hoeffler. 1992. *Telephone-Based Fraud: A survey of the American Public*. New York: Louis Harris & Associates, Inc.

Baumol, William. 1993. *Entrepreneurship, Management, and the Structure of Payoff*. Cambridge, MA: MIT Press.

Becker, Howard S. 1982. *Art Worlds*. Berkeley and Los Angeles: University of California Press.

————. 1998. *Tricks of the Trade*. Chicago: University of Chicago Press.

Bergier, Jacques. 1975. *Secret Armies: the growth of corporate and industrial espionage*. Translated by Harold J. Salemson. Indianapolis: Bobbs-Merrill.

Beren, Alex. 2007. "CA report lambastes founder." *New York Times*, April 17: B1, B4.

Best, Joel, and David F. Luckenbill. 1982. *Organizing Deviance*. Englewood Cliffs, NJ: Prentice-Hall Inc.

Bittner, Egon. 1967. "The police on skid-row: a study of peace keeping." *American Sociological Review* 32: 699–715.

Bizjak, John M., and Michael L. Lemmon. 2007. "Option backdating and board interlocks." *Review of Financial Studies* 22: 4821–47.

Black, William K. 2000. "Control fraud and control freaks." In *Contemporary Issues in Crime and Criminal Justice*, ed. Henry N. Pontell and David Shichor, 67–80. Upper Saddle River, NJ: Prentice Hall.

Blundell, William E. 1977. *Swindled*. New York: Dow Jones Books.

Boffey, Philip. 1986. "Rocket Engineers tell of pressure for a launching." *New York Times*, February 26: A1.

Bogdanich, Walt. 2007. "Senate report says SEC botched hedge fund inquiry." *New York Times*, February 2: C1–2.

Boulton, David. 1978. *The Grease Machine*. New York: Harper & Row.

Bourdieu, P. 1980. "Le capital social: notes provisoires." *Actes de la Recherche en Sciences Sociales* 31: 2–3.

Bourdieu, P., and L. J. D. Wacquant. 1992. "The purpose of reflexive sociology." In *An Invitation to Reflexive Sociology*, 61–215. Chicago: University of Chicago Press.

Bradach, Jeffrey L., and Robert G. Eccles. 1989. "Price, authority, and trust: from ideal types to plural forms." *Annual Review of Sociology* 15: 97–118.

Breiger, Ronald L. 1974. "The duality of persons and groups." *Social Forces* 53: 181–90.

Browning, Lynnley. 2007. "Four men, but not Ernst & Young, are charged in tax shelter case." *New York Times*, May 31: C3.

Bryant, Peter G., and E. Woodraw Eckard. 1991. "Price Fixing: The Probability of Getting Caught." *Review of Economics and Statistics* 73: 531–7.

Bryce, Robert. 2002. *Pipe Dreams*. New York: Public Affairs.

Burt, Ronald J. 1988. "The stability of American markets." *American Journal of Sociology* 93: 356–95.

———. 1992. *Structural Holes: The Social Structure of Competition*. Cambridge, MA: Harvard University Press.

———. 1993. "Market Integration." In *Interdisciplinary Perspectives of Organization Studies*, ed. Siegwart M. Lindenberg and Hein Schreuder, 241–92. New York: Pergamon Press.

Burton, M. Diane, and Christine M. Beckman. 2007. "Leaving a legacy: position imprints and successor turnover in young firms." *American Sociological Review* 72: 239–66.

Calavita, Kitty, and Henry N. Pontell. 1990. "Heads I win, tails you lose." *Crime & Delinquency* 36: 309–41.

Calavita, Kitty, Henry N. Pontell, and R. Tillman. 1997. *Big Money Crime: Fraud and Politics in the Savings and Loan Crisis*. Berkeley: University of California Press.

Carruthers, B., and W. Espeland. 1991. "Accounting for rationality: double-entry bookkeeping and the rhetoric of economic rationality." *American Journal of Sociology* 97: 31–69.

Chancellor, Edward. 1999. *Devil Take the Hindmost: A History of Financial Speculation*. New York: Farrar, Straus, Giroux.

Cicourel, Aaron V. 1968. *The Social Organization of Juvenile Justice*. New York: John Wiley & Sons, Inc.

Clark, Nicola. 2008. "In Europe, New scrutiny of ethnical standards." *New York Times*, May 7: C8.

Clinard, Marshall B. 1983. *Corporate Ethics and Crime: The Role of Middle Managements*. Beverly Hills: Sage.

———. 1984. "Review of Michael Levi. The Phantom Capitalists: The Organization and Control of Long-firm Fraud." *British Journal of Sociology* 35: 141–3.

Clinard, Marshall B., and Peter C. Yeager. 1980. *Corporate Crime*. New York: Macmillan.

Coase, Ronald H. 1988. "The First, the Market, and the Law." In *The Firm, the Market, and the Law*, ed. R. H. Coase, 1–31. Chicago: University of Chicago Press.

Cole, Benjamin M. 2007. *Regulatory Targeting During Times of Corporate Scandals: How social discourse influences the norms of punishment and creates a liability of status*. Manuscript. Ann Arbor, MI: University of Michigan, Stephen M. Ross School of Business.

Coleman, James S. 1974. *Power and the Structure of Society*. Philadelphia: University of Philadelphia Press.

———. 1988. "Social capital in the creation of human capital." *American Journal of Sociology* 94: S95–S120.

———. 1990. *The Foundations of Social Action*. Cambridge, MA: Harvard University Press.

Coleman, James William. 1987. "Toward an integrated theory of white-collar crime." *American Journal of Sociology* 93: 406–39.

Connor, John. 1997. "Archer Daniels Midland: Price-fixing to the world." In *Agricultural Economics Staff Papers*, vol. 4. Purdue University.

Creed, Douglas W. E., James Langstraat, and Maureen Scully. 2002. "A picture of the frame: Frame analysis as a technique and as politics." *Organizational Research Methods* 5: 34–55.

Cressey, Donald R. 1953. *Other People's Money: A Study in the Social Psychology of Embezzlement*. Glencoe, IL: Free Press.

———. 2001. "The poverty of theory in corporate crime research." In *Crimes of Privilege: Readings in White Collar Crime*, ed. Neal Shover and John Paul Wright, 175–194. New York: Oxford University Press.

Creswell, Julie. 2009. "Oh, no? What happened to Archway?" *New York Times*, May 31: Sunday Business, B1, B6.

Czarniawska-Joerges, B. 1997. *Narrating the Organization: Dramas of Institutional Identity*. Chicago: University of Chicago Press.

Dash, Eric. 2007. "Citigroup's revamp may trim its compliance corps." *New York Times*, April 10: C9.

———. 2007. "No charges for Apple over options." *New York Times*, April 25: C1, C10.

———. 2008. "Citigroup Resolves Claims That It Helped Enron Deceive Investors." *i*, March 27: C3.

Davidson, Wallace N., and Dan L. Worrell. 1988. "The Impact of Announcements of Corporate Illegalities on Shareholder Returns." *The Academy of Management Journal* 31: 195–200.

DeFranco, Edward J. 1973. *Anatomy of a Scam: A Case Study of a Planned Bankruptcy by Organized Crime*. Washington, DC: U.S. Government Printing Office.

De la Pradelle, Michele. 2006. *Market Day in Provence*. Translated by Amy Jacobs. Chicago: University of Chicago Press.

Della Porta, Donatella, and Alberto Vannucci. 1999. *Corrupt Exchanges: Actors, Resources, and Mechanisms of Political Corruption*. New York: Aldine De Gruyter.

Dempsey, Judy. 2009. "Bribery Inquiry at Manufacturer Man." *New York Times*, May 13: B8.

Dickinson, Tim. 2008. "Make-Believe Maverick." *Rolling Stone*, October 16: 56–58, 60, 62, 64–70, 72, 87.

DiFonzo, Nicholas. 2008. *The Watercooler Effect*. New York: Penguin Group.

DiMaggio, Paul. 1987. "Classification in art." *American Sociological Review* 52: 440–55.

———. 1991. "Constructing an organizational field as a professional project: U.S. art museums, 1920–1940." In *The New Institutionalism in Organizational Analysis*, ed. Walter W. Powell and Paul J. DiMaggio, 27–292. Chicago: University of Chicago Press.

————. 1994. "Culture and economy." In *The Handbook of Economic Sociology*, ed. Neil Smelser and Richard Swedberg, 27–57. Princeton: Princeton University Press.

DiMaggio, Paul, and Hugh Louch. 1998. "Socially embedded transactions: For what kinds of purchases do people most often use networks?" *American Sociological Review* 63: 619–37.

DiMaggio, Paul and Walter Powell. 1983. "The iron cage revisited: institutional isomorphism and collective rationality in organizational fields." *American Sociological Review* 48: 147–60.

Dobbin, Frank, and John R. Sutton. 1998. "The Strength of a Weak State: The Rights Revolution and the Rise of Human Resources Management Divisions." *American Journal of Sociology* 104: 441–76.

Durkheim, Emile. [1893] 1947. *The Division of Labor in Society*. New York: Free Press.

————. [1895] 1938. *The Rules of the Sociological Method*. New York: Free Press.

————. [1912] 1995. *The Elementary Forms of Religious Life*. Translated by K. E. Fields. New York: Free Press.

Edelhertz, Herbert. 1970. *The Nature, Impact and Prosecution of White-Collar Crime*. Washington, DC: U.S. Department of Justice, Law Enforcement Assistance Administration.

Edelman, Lauren B. 1992. "Legal ambiguity and symbolic structures: organizational mediation of Civil Rights Law." *American Journal of Sociology* 97: 1531–76.

Edelman, Lauren B,. and Mark C. Suchman. 1997. "The legal environments of organizations." *Annual Review of Sociology* 23: 479–515.

Edelman, Lauren B., Christopher Uggen, and Howard S. Erlanger. 1999. "The endogeneity of legal regulation: grievance procedures as rational myth." *American Journal of Sociology* 105: 406–54.

Eichenwald, Kurt. 1995. *Serpent on the Rock*. New York: Harper Collins.

————. 2002. *The Informant*. New York: Broadway Books.

————. 2005. *Conspiracy of Fools*. New York: Broadway Books.

Eisenberg, Theodore, and Jonathan R. Macey. 2004. "Was Arthur Andersen Different? An Empirical Examination of Major Accounting Firm Audits of Large Clients." *Journal of Empirical Legal Studies* 1 (2): 263–300.

Elliot, Larry A., and Richard J. Schroth. 2002. *How Companies Lie: Why Enron is Just the Tip of The Iceberg*. New York: Crown Business.

Entman, Robert M. 1991. "Framing U.S. coverage of international news: Contrasts in narratives of the KAL and Iran air incidents." *Journal of Communication* 41: 6–27.

Erickson, Bonnie H. 1996. "The structure of ignorance." *Connections* 19: 28–38.

Erikson, Kai. T. 1966. *Wayward Puritans: A Study in the Sociology of Deviance*. New York: John Wiley & Sons, Inc.

Etzioni, Amitai. 1985. "The political economy of imperfect competition." *Journal of Public Policy* 5: 169–86.

Ezell, Michael E., Kenneth C. Land, and Lawrence E. Cohen. 2003. "Modeling multiple failure time data: a survey of variance-corrected proportional hazards models with empirical applications to arrest data." In *Sociological Methodology 2003: Volume 33*, 111–67. Oxford: Blackwell Publishing for The American Sociological Association.

Faulkner, Robert R. 2002. "Our Turn." *Accounts: A Newsletter of Economic Sociology* 3: 2–4.

———. 2008. "Repertoires of Wrongdoing in Markets." The Dean's Lecture. Institute of Economics and Sociology. University of Lodz, Poland.

———. 2009. "Is Being Bad Good For Business? Market Responses to Announced Allegations of Economic Crime by Corporations." Working Paper. Social and Demographic Research Institute. University of Massachusetts, Amherst.

Faulkner, Robert R., and Howard S. Becker. 2009. *"Do You Know…?" The Jazz Repertoire in Action*. Chicago: University of Chicago Press.

Faulkner, Robert, and Eric Cheney. 2004. "The jazz repertoire." Les mondes du jazz aujord/hui. *Sociologie de L'art*, nouvelle serie—opus 8: 15–26.

———. 2011. "The social organization of defection: secret networks and the collapse of Watergate, 1971–1973." Working Paper. Social and Demographic Research Institute, University of Massachusetts, Amherst.

Faulkner, Robert R., Eric R. Cheney, Gene A. Fisher, and Wayne E. Baker. 2003. "Crime by Committee: conspirators and company men in the illegal electrical industry cartel, 1954–1959." *Criminology* 41: 511–54.

Fidler, Stephen, and Andrew England. 2007. "'People could die': how the inquiry into BAE's Saudi deals was brought to earth." *Financial Times*, February 26: 13.

Fligstein, N. 1996. "Markets as politics: a political-cultural approach to market institutions." *American Sociological Review* 61: 656–73.

Fox, Loren. 2003. *Enron: The Rise and Fall*. New York: John Wiley & Sons, Inc.

Freidson, Eliot. 1975. *Doctoring Together: A Study of Professional Social Control*. New York: Elsevier.

Friedland, Roger, and John Mohr. 2004. *Matters of Culture. Cultural Sociology in Practice*. New York: Cambridge University Press.

Freidson, Eliot, and Buford Rhea. 1963. "Processes of control in a company of equals." *Social Problems* 11: 119–31.

Fukuyama, Francis. 1995. *Trust: the social virtues and the creation of prosperity*. London: Penguin.

Furnivall, J. S. 1948. *Colonial Policy and Practice: A Comparative Study of Burma and Netherlands India*. London: Cambridge University Press.

Galanter, Marc. 1983. "Reading the landscape of disputes: what we know and don't know (and think we know) about our allegedly contentious and litigious society." *UCLA Law Review* 31 (4): 4–71.

Gamson, William A. 1992. *Talking Politics*. Cambridge: Cambridge University Press.

Gamson, William A., and Andre Modigliani. 1987. "The Changing Culture of Affirmative Action." *Research in Political Sociology* 3: 137–77.

Gambetta, Diego. 1990. Trust: *The Making and Breaking of Cooperative Relations*. Oxford: Blackwell.

———. 1993. *The Sicilian Mafia: The Business of Private Protection*. Cambridge, MA: Harvard University Press.

Gandossy, Robert P. 1985. *Bad Business: The OPM Scandal and the Seduction of the Establishment*. New York: Basic Books, Inc.

Garfinkel, Harold. 1956. "Conditions of successful degradation ceremonies." *American Journal of Sociology* 61: 420–4.

Geis, Gilbert. 2007. *White-Collar and Corporate Crime*. Upper Saddle River, NJ: Pearson Prentice Hall.

Geis, Gilbert, and Robert Meier, eds. 1977. *White Collar Crime, Offense in Business, Politics and the Professions*. Revised ed. New York: The Free Press.

Geis, Gilbert, Paul Jesilow, Henry Pontell, and Mary Jane O'Brien. 1985. "Fraud and abuse by psychiatrists against government medical benefit programs." *American Journal of Psychiatry* 142: 231–4.

Ghaziani, Amin, and Marc J. Ventressa. 2005. "Keywords and Cultural Change: Frame Analysis of Business Model Public Talk, 1975–2000." *Sociological Forum* 20: 523–59.

Glaser, Barney, and Anselm L. Strauss. 1964. "Awareness contexts and social interaction." *American Sociological Review* 29: 669–79.

———. 1965. *Awareness of Dying*. Chicago: Aldine.

Glater, Jonathan D. 2008. "Wave of Lawsuits over losses could hit a wall." *New York Times*, May 8: C1, C12.

Gluckman, Max. 1963. "Gossip and scandal." *Current Anthropology* 4: 307–16.

Goodenough, Ward H. 1981. *Culture, Language, and Society*. Menlo Park, CA: Benjamin/Cummings Publishing Company, Inc.

Granovetter, Mark S. 1985. "Economic action and social structure: the problem of embeddedness." *American Journal of Sociology* 91: 481–510.

Gray, Wayne B., and John T. Scholz. 1993. "Does regulatory enforcement work? A panel analysis of OSHA enforcement." *Law & Society Review* 27: 177–214.

Gray, Wayne B., and Ronald J. Shadbegian. 2005. "When and why do plants comply? Paper Mills in the 1980s." *Law and Policy* 27: 238–61.

Gross, Martin. 1996. *The Political Racket: Deceit, Self Interest and Corruption in American Politics*. New York: Ballentine.

Hagerty, James R., and Evan Perez. 2009. "FBI Looks Into Losses At Freddie." *Wall Street Journal*, April 30: C3.

Hamilton, Peter. 1967. *Espionage and Subversion in an Industrial Society*. London: Hutchinson.

Hartocollis, Anemona, and Larry Rohter. 2007. "Brazilian politician indicted in New York in kickback scheme." *New York Times*, March 9: A9.

Hayward, Mathew L. A., and Warren Boeker. 1998. "Power and conflicts of interest in professional firms: evidence from investment banking." *Administrative Science Quarterly* 43: 1–22.

Heckman, James, and Burton Singer. 1984. "A method for minimizing the impact of distributional assumptions in econometric models for duration data." *Econometrica* 52: 271–320.

Helft, Miguel. 2009. "Unwritten code rules Silicon Valley hiring." *New York Times*, June 4: B11.

Henriques, Diana B. 2009. "Financier Sued Over Madoff Ties." *New York Times*, April 7: B1, B4.

Herling, John. 1962. *The Great Price Conspiracy: The Story of the Antitrust Violations in the Electrical Industry*. Washington, DC: Robert B. Luce.

Hersh, Seymour. 2001. "The price of oil: what was Mobil up to in Kazakhstan and Russia?" *New Yorker*, July 9: 48–65.

Hirsch, Paul, and Jo-Ellen Pozner. 2005. "To avoid surprises, acknowledge the dark side: illustrations from securities analysts." *Strategic Organization* 3: 229–38.

Hirschman, Albert O. 1970. *Exit, Voice and Loyalty: Responses to Decline in Firms, Organizations, and States.* Cambridge, MA: Harvard University Press.

———. 1997. *The Dark Side of Camelot.* Boston: Little Brown and Company.

Hirsh, C. Elizabeth. 2009. "The strength of weak enforcement: the impact of discrimination charges, legal environments, and organizational conditions of workplace segregation." *American Sociological Review* 74: 245–71.

Hirsh, Michael. 2008. "Mortgages and Madness." *Newsweek,* June 2: 38–40.

Holsti, Ole R. 1968. "Content analysis." In *The Handbook of Social Psychology. Volume Two,* ed. Gardner Lindzey and Elliot Aronson, 596–692. Reading, MA: Addison-Wesley Publishing Company.

———. 1969. *Content Analysis for the Social Sciences and Humanities.* Reading, MA: Addison-Wesley Publishing Company.

Hopkins, Keith. 1993. "Novel evidence for Roman slavery." *Past and Present* 138: 1–13.

Hsu, Greta, Michael T. Hannan, and Ozgecan Kocak. 2009. "Multiple Category memberships in markets: An integrative theory and two empirical tests." *American Sociological Review* 74: 150–69.

Jacoby, Neil H., Peter Hehemkis, and Richard Eells. 1977. *Bribery and Extortion in World Business.* New York: Macmillan.

Jonsson, Stefan, Henrich R. Greve, and Takako Fujiwara-Greve. 2009. "Undeserved Loss: The spread of legitimacy loss to innocent organizations in response to reported corporate deviance." *Administrative Science Quarterly* 54: 195–228.

Karpoff, J. M., and J. R. Lott, Jr. 1993. "The Reputation Penalty Firms Bear from Committing Criminal Fraud." *Journal of Law and Economics* 36: 757–802.

Katz, Jack. 1977. "Cover-up and collective integrity." *Social Problems* 25: 3–17.

———. 1988. *Seductions of Crime.* New York: Basic Books.

Kitchens, Thomas L. 1993. "The cash flow analysis method: following the paper trail in Ponzi schemes." *FBI Law Enforcement Bulletin* August, 10–13.

Klein, B., Crawford, R. G., and Alchain, A. A. 1978. "Vertical Integration, Appropriable Rents and the Competitive Contracting Process." *Journal of Law and Economics* 21: 297–326.

Klinenberg, Eric. 2002. *Heat Wave: A Social Autopsy of Disaster in Chicago.* Chicago: University of Chicago Press.

Krippendorff, Klaus. 1980. *Content Analysis: An Introduction to Its Methodology.* Newbury Park, CA: Sage.

Labaton, Stephen. 2009. "Administration will strengthen antitrust rules." *New York Times,* May 11: front page, A3.

Leach, Jerry W. 1983. *The Kula: New Perspectives on Massim Exchange.* New York: Cambridge University Press.

Lean, David F., Jonathan D. Ogur, and Robert P. Rogers. 1982. "Competition and collusion in electrical equipment markets." In Bureau of Economics Staff Report to the Federal Trade Commission. Washington, DC: Bureau of Economics.

Ledeneva, A. V. 1998. *Russia's Economy of Favours: Blat, Networking and Informal Exchange.* Cambridge: Cambridge University Press.

Leifer, Eric M. 1985. "Markets as mechanisms: using a role structure." *Social Forces* 64: 442–72.

Levine, Dennis B. 1991. *Inside Out: An Insider's Account of Wall Street*. New York: G. P. Putnam's Sons.

Lévi-Strauss, Claude. [1949] 1969. *The Elementary Structures of Kinship*. Boston: Beacon Press.

Levitt, Arthur with Paula Dwyer. 2002. *Take on the Street: What Wall Street and Corporate America Don't Want You to Know; What You Can Do to Fight Back*. New York: Random House.

Levitz, Jennifer. 2010. "State street probe examines whether firm misled clients." *Wall Street Journal*, April 30: C1.

Lichtblau, Eric. 2008. "In justice shift, corporate deals replace trials." *New York Times*, April 9: page 1, A20.

———. 2008. "Mukasey Declines to Create a U.S. Task Force to Investigate Mortgage Fraud." *New York Times*, June 6: C4.

Lieber, James B. 2002. *Rats in the Grain: The Dirty Tricks and Trials of Archer Daniels Midland, the Supermarket to the World*. New York: Four Walls Eight Windows.

Lohr, Steve, 2007. "Oracle says rival stole its software." *New York Times*, March 23: C1, 7.

Long, J. S. 1997. *Regression Models for Categorical and Limited Dependent Variables*. Thousand Oaks, CA: Sage.

Lukawitz, James. M., and Paul John Steinbart. 1995. "Investor Reaction to Disclosures of Employee Fraud." *Journal of Managerial Issues* 7: 358–62.

Lusk, Harold F., Charles M. Hewitt, John D. Donnell, and A. James Barnes. 1970. *Business Law: Principles and Cases*. Homewood, IL: Richard D. Irwin, Inc.

Macaulay, Stuart. 1963. "Non-contractual relations in business: a preliminary study." *American Sociological Review* 28: 55–67.

Machiavelli, Niccolo. [1532] 1955. *The Prince*. Translated by David Wootton. Indianapolis: Hackett Publishing Company, Inc.

Mahar, Maggie. 2003. *Bull!: A History of the Boom, 1982–1999: What Drove the Breakneck Market—and What Every Investor Needs to Know About Financial Cycles*. New York: HarperCollins.

Malinowski, Bronislaw. 1922. *Argonauts of the Western Pacific*. London: Routledge.

Manuel, Dave. 2009. "Is the SEC corrupt, inept or both?" davemanuel.com, June 10.

March, James G. 1991. "Exploration and exploitation in organizational learning." *Organization Science* 2: 71–87.

Mason, Christopher. 2004. *Art of the Steal: Inside the Sotheby's-Christie's Auction House Scandal*. New York: Putnam Publishing Group.

McChesney, Fred. 1997. *Money for Nothing: Politicians, Rent Extraction, and Political Extortion*. Cambridge, MA: Harvard University Press.

McLean, Bethany, and Peter Elkind. 2003. *The Smartest Guys in the Room: The Amazing Rise and Scandalous Fall of Enron*. New York: Penguin.

McLean, Paul. D. 1998. "A frame analysis of favor seeking in the Renaissance: agency, networks, and political culture." *American Journal of Sociology* 104: 51–91.

Meier, Barry, and Jad Mouawad. 2007. "No oil yet, but tiny African isle finds dealings just as slippery." *New York Times*, July 2: front page, A8.

Meyer, J. W., and B. Rowan. 1977. "Institutionalized organizations: formal structure as myth and ceremony." *American Journal of Sociology* 83: 340–63.

———. 1978. "The structure of educational Organizations." In *Environments and Organizations*, ed. John W. Meyer, 78–109. San Francisco: Jossey Bass.

Michaely, R., and K. L. Womack. 1999. "Conflict of interest and the credibility of underwriter analyst recommendations." *Review of Financial Studies* 12: 653–86.

Miller, Norman C. 1965. *The Great Salad Oil Swindle*. New York: Coward McCann.

Mizrachi, Nissim, Israel Drori, and Reneer Anspach. 2007. "Repertoires of trust: the practice of trust in a multinational organization amid political conflict." *American Sociological Review* 72: 143–65.

Mnookin, Robert, and Lewis Kornhauser. 1979. "Bargaining in the shadow of the law: The case of divorce." *Yale Law Journal* 88 (5): 950–97.

Molotch, Harvey, and Marilyn Lester. 1974. "News as purposive behavior: on the strategic use of routine events, accidents, and scandals." *American Sociological Review* 39: 101–21.

Morgenson, Gretchen. 2007. "Making managers pay, literally." *New York Times*, March 25: Sunday Business Section 3, 1, 10.

———. 2008. "Suit Claims UBS Misled Investors." *New York Times*, June 27: C1, C6.

Murphy, Gregory L. 2004. *The Big Book of Concepts*. Cambridge, MA: MIT Press.

New York State Organized Crime Task Force. 1988. *Corruption and Racketeering in the New York City Construction Industry*. Ithaca, NY: Cornell University School of Labor and Industrial Relations.

Norris, Floyd. 2007. "Baker Hughes admits to overseas bribery." *New York Times*, April 27: C5.

Palmer, Donald. 1983. "Broken ties: Interlocking directorates and intercorporate coordination." *Administrative Science Quarterly* 28: 40–55.

Partnoy, Frank. 2009. *The Match King: Ivar Kreuger, the Financial Genius Behind a Century of Wall Street Scandals*. New York: Public Affairs.

Pear, Robert. 1985. "Paradyne penalty proposed." *New York Times*, March 13: Section D, page 4.

Peters, Jeremy W., and Nick Bunkley. 2007. "Stockman is charged with fraud." *New York Times*, March 27: C1, 6.

Pedriana, Nicholas, and Robin Stryker. 2004. "The Strength of a Weak Agency: Enforcement of Title VII of the 1964 Civil Rights Act and the Expansion of State Capacity, 1965–1971." *American Journal of Sociology* 110: 709–60.

Pfeffer, J., and P. Nowak. 1976. "Joint ventures and interorganizational interdependence." *Administrative Science Quarterly* 21: 398–418.

Pilzer, Paul Zane. 1989. *Other People's Money*. New York: Simon & Schuster.

Pizzo, Stephen, Mary Fricker, and Paul Muolo. 1989. *Inside Job: The Looting of America's Savings and Loans*. New York: McGraw Hill.

Podolny, J. M. 1993. "A status-based model of market competition." *American Journal of Sociology* 98: 829–72.

———. 2001. "Networks as the Pipes and Prisms of the Market." *American Journal of Sociology* 107: 33–60.

Porac, J. F., J. B. Wade, and T. G. Pollock. 1999. "Industry categories and the politics of the comparable firm in CEO compensation." *Administrative Science Quarterly* 44: 112–44.

Porter, Michael E. 1990. *Competitive Strategy: Techniques for Analyzing Industries and Competitors.* New York: The Free Press.

Poovey, Mary. 1998. *History of the Modern Fact.* Chicago: University of Chicago Press.

Powers, D. A., and Y. Xie. 2000. *Statistical Methods for Categorical Data Analysis.* San Diego, CA: Academic Press.

Preuschat, Archibald. 2009. "Siemens takes more steps to settle bribery scandal." *Wall Street Journal: European,* July 3–5: 7.

Ragin, Charles. 1994. *Constructing Social Research: The Unity and Diversity of Method.* Newbury Park, CA: Sage.

Reisman, Michael. 1979. *Folded Lies: Bribery, Crusades and Reforms.* New York: Free Press.

Reskin, Barbara F. 2001. "Employment Discrimination and its Remedies." In *Sourcebook of Labor Markets: Evolving Structures and Processes,* ed. I. Berg and A. L. Kallenberg, 567–600. New York: Plenum.

Rindova, V. P., T. G. Pollock, and M. L. Hayward. 2006. "Celebrity firms: the social construction of market popularity." *Academy of Management Review* 31: 50–71.

Rosnow, Ralph L., and Gary Alan Fine. 1976. *Rumor and Gossip: The Social Psychology of Hearsay.* New York: Elsevier.

Ross, Irwin. 1980. "How lawless are big companies?" *Fortune,* December 1: 57–64.

Rosoff, Stephen M., Henry N. Pontell, and Robert H. Tilman. 2007. *Profit Without Honor: White-Collar Crime and the Looting of America.* Upper Saddle River, NJ: Pearson/Prentice Hall.

Salop, Steven C. 1981. *Strategy, Predation, and Antitrust Analysis.* Washington: Federal Trade Commission Bureau of Economics Bureau of Competition.

Schilit, Howard. 2002. *Financial Shenanigans: How to Detect Accounting Gimmicks and Fraud in Financial Reports.* New York: McGraw-Hill.

Schubert, S., and T. C. Miller. 2009. "At Siemens bribery was just a line item." *Frontline World,* February 13.

Schumpeter, Joseph. 1934. *The Theory of Economic Development.* Cambridge, MA: Harvard University Press.

Schwartz, Nelson D. 2007. "Who might escape Bausch without a scratch?" *New York Times,* June 24: Business Section 3: 1, 8.

Scott, W. Richard, and John W. Meyer. 1978. "The organization of societal sectors: propositions and early evidence." In *Environments and Organizations,* ed. John W. Meyer, 108–40. San Francisco: Jossey-Bass.

Seal, Mark. 2009. "Bernie Madoff's private world: The money, the madness, and the mysteries." *Vanity Fair,* June, 96–106, 158–63.

Sewell, William J. 1992. "A theory of structure: duality, agency, and transformation." *American Journal of Sociology* 91: 1–19.

———. 1999. "The Concept of Culture." In *Beyond the Cultural Turn: New Directions in the Study of Society and Culture,* ed. Victoria E. Bonnell and Lynn Hunt, 35–61. Berkeley, CA: University of California Press.

Shapiro. Susan P. 1980. *Thinking About White Collar Crimes.* Washington, DC: U.S. Department of Justice. National Institute of Justice.

———. 1984. *Wayward Capitalists: Target of the Securities and Exchange Commission.* New Haven and London: Yale University Press.

———. 1990. "Collaring the crime, not the criminal: Reconsidering the concept of white-collar crime." *American Sociological Review* 55: 346–65.

Shibutani, Tamotsu. 1966. *Improvised News: A Sociological Study of Rumor*. Indianapolis: Bobbs-Merrill.

Siconolfi, Michael, William Power, Laurie P. Cohen, and Robert Guenther. 1990. "Rise and fall: Wall Street era ends as Drexel Burnham decides to liquidate." *Wall Street Journal*, February 14: A1, A6.

Simon, David R., and Frank E. Hagan. 1999. *White-Collar Deviance*. Boston: Allyn & Bacon.

Sims, G. Thomas. 2007. "Siemens chief agrees to quit in scandal." *New York Times*, April 26: C1, 14.

Skinner, Quentin. 1990. "Thomas Hobbes: Rhetoric and the Construction of Morality." *Proceedings of the British Academy* 76: 1–61.

Skolnick, Jerome H. 1980. *House of Cards: Legalization and Control of Casino Gambling*. Boston: Little, Brown and Company.

Slobodzian, Joseph A. 1997. "New Era Founder Pleads No Contest." *Philadelphia Inquirer,* March 1: 27.

Smith, Richard Austin. 1961. "The Incredible Electrical Conspiracy Part I." *Fortune* 63: 132–7, 161–4.

Snow, Robert P. 1978. "The Golden Fleece: Arizona Land Fraud." In *Crime at The Top*, ed. John M. Johnson and Jack D. Douglas, 133–50. Philadelphia: J.B. Lippincott Company.

Sonnefeld, Jeffrey, and Paul R. Lawrence. 1978. "Why do companies succumb to price-fixing?" *Harvard Business Review*, July–August: 145–57.

Stevenson, Robert. 1998. *The Boiler Room and Other Telephone Sales Scams*. Champagne, IL: University of Illinois Press.

Stewart, James. B. 1992. *Den of Thieves*. New York: Simon & Schuster.

———. 2001. "Bidding War." *New Yorker*, October 15: 158–75.

———. 2007. "The Kona files: Hewlett-Packard's surveillance scandal." *New Yorker*, February 19: 152–67.

Stiglitz, Joseph E. 2003. *The Roaring Nineties*. New York: W.W. Norton & Company Ltd.

Stinchcombe, Arthur L. 1990. *Information and Organizations*. Berkeley: University of California Press.

Strader, J. Kelly. 2006. *Understanding White Collar Crime*. Newark, NJ: LexisNexis/Matthew Bender & Company, Inc.

Sutherland, Edwin H. 1940. "White-collar criminality." *American Sociological Review* 5: 1–11.

———. 1949 [1983]. *White Collar Crime: The Uncut Version*. New Haven, CT: Yale University Press.

Swedberg, Richard. 1987. "Economic Sociology: Past and Present." *Current Sociology: la sociologie contemporaine* 35 (1).

———. 1994. "Markets as social structure." In *The Handbook of Economic Sociology*, ed. Neil Smelser and Richard Swedberg, 255–82. Princeton: Princeton University Press.

———. 2003. *Principles of Economic Sociology*. Princeton: Princeton University Press.

Swidler, A. 1986. "Culture in action: symbols and strategies." *American Sociological Review* 51: 273–86.

———. 2003. *Talk of Love: How Culture Matters*. Chicago: University of Chicago Press.

Thomas, W. I., and F. Znaniecki. 1918. *The Polish Peasant in Europe and America: Monograph of an Immigrant Group*. Boston: Badger.

Tillman, Robert, and Michael Indergaard. 1999. "Field of schemes: Health insurance fraud in the small business sector." *Social Problems* 46: 572–90.

Tilly, Charles. 1985. "War making and state making as organized crime." In *Bringing the State Back In*, ed. Dietrich Rueschemeyer and Theda Skocpol, 169–91. Cambridge: Cambridge University Press.

———. 1995a. *Popular Contention in Great Britain, 1758–1834*. Cambridge, MA: Harvard University Press.

———. 1995b. "Contentious repertoires in Great Britain, 1758–1834." In *Repertoires and Cycles of Collective Action*, ed. Mark Traugott, 15–42. Durham, NC: Duke University Press.

———. 2006. *Why? What Happens When People Give Reasons…and Why*. Princeton: Princeton University Press.

Tomaskovic-Devey, Donald, Catherine Zimmer, Sandra Harding, and Dustin Avent-Holt. 2007. "Profits trust and contract: the simultaneity of market, hierarchy and network principles." Manuscript. Amherst, MA: University of Massachusetts, Department of Sociology.

Trouillot, Michel-Rolph. 1995. *Silencing the Past: Power and the Production of History*. Boston: Beacon Press.

Tuchman, Gaye. 1973. "Making news by doing work: routinizing the unexpected." *American Journal of Sociology* 79: 110–31.

Turnaturi, Gabriella. 2007. *Betrayals: The Unpredictability of Human Relations*. Translated by Lydia G. Cochrane. Chicago: University of Chicago Press.

Turner, Jonathan H, Leonard Beeghley, and Charles H. Powers. 2002. *The Emergence of Sociological Theory*. Belmont, CA: Wadsworth Thompson Learning.

Turner, Ralph H., and Lewis M. Killian. 1957. *Collective Behavior*. Englewood, NJ: Prentice-Hall.

Turner, Ralph H. and Samuel J. Surace. 1957. "Zoot-suiters and Mexicans: Symbols in crowd behavior." In *Collective Behavior*, ed. Ralph H. Turner and Lewis M. Killian, 122–9. Englewood, NJ: Prentice-Hall.

Utah Department of Commerce. 2007. "Media Alert." December 31. http://www.securities.utah.gov/press/topscams2008.pdf (accessed May 2011).

Velho, Gilberto. 1976. "Accusations, family mobility and deviant behavior." *Sociology Problems* 23: 268–75.

Vaughan, Diane. 1996. "Anomie theory and organizations: culture and the normalization of deviance at NASA." In *The Future of Anomie Theory*, ed. Nikos Passas and Robert Ages, 95–123. Boston: Northeastern University Press.

———. 1999. "The dark side of organizations: Mistake, misconduct, and disaster." *Annual Review of Sociology* 25: 271–305.

Vaughan, Diane, and Giovanna Carlo. 1975. "The appliance repairman: A study of victim-responsiveness and fraud." *Journal of Research in Crime and Delinquency* 12: 153–61.

Wade, J. B., J. F. Porac, and T. G. Pollock. 1997. "Worth, Words, and the Justification of Executive Pay." *Journal of Organizational Behavior* 18: 641–64.

Wallerstein, Immanuel. 2004. "The modern world-system as a capitalist world-economy." *World-Systems Analysis: An Introduction*. Durham, NC: Duke University Press.

Walton, John. 2001. *Storied Land: Community and Memory in Monterey*. Berkeley and Los Angeles: University of California Press.

Warner, K., and H. Molotch. 1993. "Information in the market-place: Media explanations of the '87 crash." *Social Problems* 40: 167–88.

Wayne, Leslie. 2004a. "Ex-Pentagon official gets 9 months for conspiring to favor Boeing." *New York Times*, October 2: B1, 13.

———. 2004b. "A growing military contract scandal: more air force deals with Boeing are questioned." *New York Times*, October 8: C1, 3–4.

———. 2009. "Money fund managers are accused of a fraud." *New York Times*, May 5: B1, 2.

Webb, Eugene J., Donald T. Campbell, Richard D. Schwartz, and Lee Sechrest. 1966. *Unobtrusive Measures: Nonreactive Research in The Social Sciences*. Chicago: Rand McNally & Company.

Weber, Robert P. 1985. *Basic Content Analysis*. Beverly Hills, CA: Sage Publications.

Weber, Max. [1922] 1978. *Economy and Society: An Outline of Interpretive Sociology*. Translated by Ephraim Fischoff et al., ed. Guenther Roth and Claus Wittich. Berkeley: University of California Press.

Weisman, Stewart L. 1999. *Need and Greed: The Story of the Largest Ponzi Scheme in American History*. Syracuse, NY: Syracuse University Press.

Wellman, Barry, and S. D. Berkowitz. 1988. *Social Structures: A Network Approach*. Cambridge: Cambridge University Press.

Werdigier, Julia, and Alan Cowell. 2008. "Court Faults Britain for Halting Arms Deal Inquiry." *New York Times*, April 11: C5.

Wheeler, Stanton, and Mitchell Rothman. 1982. "The organization as weapon in white-collar crime." *Michigan Law Review* 80: 1403–26.

White, Harrison. 1981. "Where do markets come from?" *American Journal of Sociology* 87: 517–47.

———. 1992. *Identity and Control: A Structural Theory of Social Action*. Princeton: Princeton University Press.

———. 1997. "Varieties of Markets." In *Social Structures: A Network Approach*, ed. Barry Wellman and Stanley Berkowitz, 226–57. Cambridge: Cambridge University Press.

———. 2002. *Markets from Networks: Socioeconomic Models of Production*. Princeton: Princeton University Press.

Whyte, William F. 1943. *Street Corner Society: The Social Structure of an Italian Slum*. Chicago: University of Chicago Press.

Williamson, Oliver. 1975. *Markets and Hierarchies: Analysis and Anti-Trust Implications*. New York: Free Press.

———. 1979. "Transaction-cost economics: The governance of contractual relations." *Journal of Law and Economics*. 22: 233–61.

———. 1985. *The Economic Institution of Capitalism*. New York: Free Press.

William, Oliver E., and William G. Ouchi. 1981. "The markets and hierarchies and visible hand perspective." In *Perspectives on Organization Design and Behavior*, ed. Andrew Van de Ven and William Joyce, 347–70, 387–90. New York: Wiley.

Winship, Christopher, and Michael Mandel. 1983. "Roles and position: A critique and extension of the blockmodeling approach." In *Sociological Methodology, 1983– 1984*, ed. S. Leinhardt, 314–44. San Francisco: Jossey-Bass.

Zelizer, V. 1988. "Beyond the polemics of the market: Establishing a theoretical and empirical agenda." *Sociological Forum* 3: 614–34.

Zey, Mary. 1993. *Banking on Fraud: Drexel, Junk Bonds, and Buyouts.* New York: Aldine De Gruyter.

Zey-Ferrell, Mary K., Mark Weaver, and O. C. Ferrell. 1982. "Predicting unethical behavior among marketing practitioners." *Human Relations* 32: 557–68.

Zonana, Victor. 1988. "Test equipment maker sues Hewlett." *Los Angeles Times*, May 19: Business, Part 4, 2.

Zuckerman, Gregory, and Kara Scannell. 2009. "Top fund to shut as firm faces probe." *Wall Street Journal*, May 28: 1.

Index

9 780857 287915